Legal Research Methods for the English-Speaking Caribbean

Legal Research Methods for the English-Speaking Caribbean

YASMIN MORAIS

HEAD OF COLLECTION SERVICES
UNIVERSITY OF THE DISTRICT OF COLUMBIA
DAVID A. CLARKE SCHOOL OF LAW

YEMISI DINA

CHIEF LAW LIBRARIAN
OSGOODE HALL LAW SCHOOL
YORK UNIVERSITY

CAROLINA ACADEMIC PRESS
Durham, North Carolina

LIBRARY OF CONGRESS CATALOGING-IN-PUBLICATION DATA

Names: Morais, Yasmin, author. | Dina, Yemisi, author.
Title: Legal research methods for the English-speaking Caribbean / Yasmin Morais and Yemisi Dina.
Description: Durham, North Carolina : Carolina Academic Press, 2024. | Includes bibliographical references and index.
Identifiers: LCCN 2023051813 | ISBN 9781531029302 (paperback) | ISBN 9781531029319 (ebook)
Subjects: LCSH: Legal research—Caribbean, English-speaking.
Classification: LCC KGL5043 .M67 2024 | DDC 340.072/0729—dc23/eng/20231108
LC record available at https://lccn.loc.gov/2023051813

Carolina Academic Press, LLC
700 Kent Street
Durham, North Carolina 27701
(919) 489-7486
www.cap-press.com

Printed in the United States of America

Contents

Foreword

Legal Research Methods for the English-Speaking Caribbean by Yasmin Morais and Yemisi Dina delivers on the promise of its title with efficiency and precision. Not only is this publication a valuable guide to Caribbean sources of law, but it also offers stimulating insight into legal processes prevailing in the region. It is thus a welcome addition to Caribbean legal scholarship and literature.

The countries that constitute the English-speaking Caribbean stretch geographically from Jamaica and Belize to the north and west, respectively, to Barbados in the east, and Trinidad and Tobago and Guyana in the south. These countries, together with the Bahamas in the northeast, number approximately twenty independent states and dependent territories. As a general matter, they share a common history of British colonialism, important cultural connections, and interrelated educational systems. Significantly, too, they also share Westminster-style constitutional arrangements and historical reliance on the English common law.

The shared roots of anglophone Caribbean countries in British cultural and constitutional traditions provide a valid starting point for legal research in the region. The researcher seeking Caribbean responses to legal questions is entitled to assume that different states and territories adopt similar approaches to various issues. But, to be sure, similarity does not necessarily imply sameness. In some instances, the approach to an issue in one territory may depart in either subtle or substantial ways from the approach taken in another. In analyzing legal questions across the Caribbean, therefore, caution is required: the risk of treating the Caribbean in monolithic terms should be avoided. One noteworthy feature of Morais and Dina's compendium is its sensitivity to the different solutions that may emerge from individual territories, with the work presenting clear and concise directions on how such solutions may be found amidst the mass of sources available across the region.

Another positive feature of Morais and Dina's work concerns its appreciation of the evolution of Caribbean law. This is reflected both in the book's treatment of legal history and of current legal questions. As to history, the researcher will find, for example, thoughtful direction on the structure and foundations of the West Indian Federation, a legislative scheme that, though lasting for only four years, has arguably left an enduring mark on aspects of Caribbean regionalism. As to current legal issues, the book provides a strong opening into matters of interest across the Caribbean. Again, by way of example, Morais and Dina offer both regional and local perspectives. At the regional level, references to the Caribbean Court of Justice are appropriately in place, but mindful of the local situation in some countries, the book also provides useful links to the Judicial Committee of the Privy Council.

In its various chapters, the book demonstrates careful attention to the sources of domestic law. Accordingly, there are chapters on national constitutions, legislation, local government arrangements, legislative history, case law, and court structures. There is, in addition, valuable direction on Caribbean treaty law and practice, including means of exploring the *travaux preparatoires* concerning some treaties as well as Community Decisions within the CARICOM, the Caribbean Community. The book commences with an informative review of legal research methods and includes in its closing sections up-to-date guidance about access to libraries with legal material in the region.

Legal Research Methods provides access to many resources that have not always been easy to find. In the recent past—prior to the dawn of the internet and commercial search engines—research into Caribbean legal issues was at best time consuming, with the researcher often having to transcend national boundaries to find primary and secondary material. So, for example, finding subsidiary legislation for various territories was challenging if pursued from a base in one's local library. And for researchers outside the region, save perhaps those from metropolitan centers, much of the Caribbean material was quite inaccessible. Some researchers would probably garner access through much-appreciated interlibrary loan facilities, but in the main they had to overcome major obstacles in the quest for authoritative sources. Today, however, much of this has changed, owing to phenomenal developments in information technology, which now allow many documentary sources to be found with relative ease. In this regard, the work of communities of librarians, from the Caribbean and beyond, deserves special mention and appreciation. Advances in information technology have created a whole new world for the legal scholar, a new world that has been undeniably reinforced for the Caribbean by Morais and Dina, among other librarians.

But while we celebrate enhanced access, a note of reservation is also in order. First, some sources of information may remain largely out of reach even in the present dispensation. This may be especially the case with respect to official local government sources in some jurisdictions. Second, with respect to many books and journal articles on the Caribbean, private researchers often face subscription fees that effectively limit access to material. And third, even where access to sources is available, the researcher may also need to seek out background information not readily available online or in texts. Researchers pursuing questions on case law matters, for example, will need to appreciate relationships among different courts as well as other constitutional issues that may be at play. On this last point, Morais and Dina are especially helpful, carefully explaining hierarchical issues pertaining to the courts.

Legal Research Methods for the English-Speaking Caribbean is an excellent compendium that will strengthen research efforts on Caribbean issues for years to come. Yasmin Morais and Yemisi Dina are to be congratulated for this publication: academics, business persons, government officials, students, and policy makers should derive great value from the painstaking research undertaken by the authors.

Stephen Vasciannie
Professor of International Law, Norman Manley Law School
University of the West Indies, Mona, and Former Ambassador of Jamaica to the United States

Acknowledgments

I want to thank Dr. Stephen Vasciannie, professor of international law, Norman Manley Law School, University of the West Indies, Mona, and former ambassador of Jamaica to the United States for writing the foreword. Special thanks also to Yemisi Dina for saying yes to the idea of this book and for her ongoing interest in promoting Caribbean legal research. She has been an amazing coauthor, and her contribution is invaluable. I am also grateful to Mr. Paul Cooper, former partner at Livingston, Alexander & Levy in Kingston, Jamaica, for my start in the legal field and for igniting my interest in law. Finally, thanks to my daughters, Mariel and Mikayla, for their support and constant encouragement. (YM)

My sincere appreciation goes to Yasmin Morais who invited me to coauthor this book. It has been a unique experience because of the opportunity to partner with her remotely.

I would like to thank all those researchers who continue to ask questions about the Caribbean region, which has motivated the need for this work.

I am grateful to my husband and my three children for putting up with my schedule while working on the book. (YD)

The authors would like to extend their sincere appreciation to Carol McGeehan, Susan Trimble, and all Carolina Academic Press editorial and marketing staff who worked on putting the manuscript together.

About the Authors

Yasmin Morais is the head of collection services at the Mason Law Library, David A. Clarke School of Law, University of the District of Columbia. She earned the degrees of BA (Spanish) and MSc (Government) from the University of the West Indies (Mona), the LLB (Hons.) from the University of London, and MLIS from the University of Toronto. She previously worked at the Georgetown University Law Library, University Health Network in Toronto, Canada, and the United Nations Development Program in Kingston, Jamaica. She was the chair of the Latin American Law Interest Group, Foreign, Comparative and International Law Section, American Association of Law Libraries from 2017 to 2019. Her research interests include institutional repositories, copyright, legal research, and foreign, international, and comparative law.

Yemisi Dina, MPPAL, MLIS, LLB, MA, is Chief Law Librarian at the Osgoode Hall Law Library, York University, Toronto, Ontario, Canada. She previously worked at the College of the Bahamas/University of the West Indies Law Program Library, Nassau, the Bahamas; The Nigerian Law School, Lagos Campus; and the Adeola Odutola Law Library, University of Ibadan, Ibadan, Nigeria. Her areas of interest and specialization include law librarianship;

information technology and its application to the delivery of information services; legal research methods; women's studies; and foreign, comparative, and international law. She teaches legal research in the JD and graduate programs.

She is an active member of the American Association of Law Libraries, Chair African Interest Group of the Foreign, Comparative and International Law Special Interest Group, Caribbean Association of Law Libraries, British and Irish Association of Law Libraries, and the Canadian Association of Law Libraries where she is currently serving on the executive board as president. In October 2022, Yemisi was named as one of Canada's Most Powerful Women: Top 100 Awards in the professional category by the Women's Executive Network (https://wxnetwork.com/page/2022Top100AwardWinners) recognizing her contribution to law librarianship.

Introduction

There have been significant developments in legal jurisprudence in the English-speaking Caribbean. In addition, physical legal structures, such as courts, regional organizations focused on the law, and law schools, have increased. While there are more opportunities for Caribbean students to pursue a legal career, there is, however, a dearth in publications on legal research methods. Between 1979 and 1989, Velma Newton, one of the most prolific Caribbean legal writers, published several books on Caribbean legal systems, legal literature, and research practices, and a bibliography of primary and secondary sources. Her publications, and those of others, have enhanced the available resources on Caribbean law. However, apart from a few research guides on Caribbean law and the Caribbean Court of Justice prepared by several law librarians, there is currently no comprehensive monograph available on legal research methods for the English-speaking Caribbean region. A book on researching the laws of the English-speaking Caribbean is therefore long overdue. While there are recent contributions to Caribbean jurisprudence and other specialized areas of law, there is a gap in authoritative resources that facilitate legal research.

There is a real need for publications of this nature, especially considering the evolving nature of Caribbean law, ongoing legal reform, and emerging legal issues that impact the Caribbean—for example the legalization of marijuana, the growing popularity and use of cryptocurrency, space tourism, and the threat of climate change. As a region, the Caribbean attracts significant foreign direct investment and, compared to its size, is a major player in regional and international organizations. The Caribbean Court of Justice, the court of last resort for many of the territories, is already more than ten years old, and its decisions are influencing Caribbean legal thought, with the waning of reliance on the Judicial Committee of the Privy Council in England.

Caribbean economies are also rapidly diversifying and becoming less dependent on tourism as the major economic engine. An increasing number of its citizens are taking advantage of technology and other online platforms such as YouTube, PayPal, and Airbnb to become entrepreneurs. This often requires researching and navigating areas of law such as contracts, copyright, entertainment, and banking, as well as emerging laws related to medical marijuana.

In the education sector, the Caribbean now boasts several institutions for the study of law: University of the West Indies (campuses in Cave Hill, Barbados, and Mona, Jamaica); University of Technology, Jamaica; University of Guyana; Truman Bodden Law School (in collaboration with the University of Liverpool) in the Cayman Islands; the Eugene Dupuch Law School in the Bahamas; and the newest, the University of the Commonwealth Caribbean, which collaborates with the University of London's International Program. Chapter 1 provides an overview of the development of Caribbean legal education and an assessment of the current status of available programs to students.

This has had a favorable impact on the training of future lawyers, especially in relation to specializations such as sports, entertainment law, and legal drafting, which are relevant to Caribbean economies. Increasing collaboration between Caribbean law schools and law schools in other regions is also a positive development. The proliferation of Caribbean primary and secondary legal materials and the changing legal landscape require a current and comprehensive resource on finding and analyzing Caribbean law.

This book aims to provide a thorough coverage of how to research the laws of the English-speaking Caribbean. The focus goes beyond the Caribbean as we have decided to include some content about foreign, comparative, and international law, and researching the laws of international organizations. We believe this approach will help Caribbean law students have a mastery of legal research beyond the region. A significant portion of the work will discuss the research process and creating research strategies. Legislative history, municipal laws, and researching regional organizations and treaties will all be examined. The work builds extensively on previous Caribbean research guides created by the authors, and is an important resource for law students, law faculty, court staff, foreign direct investors, and persons interested in foreign and comparative law research.

The jurisdictions of the English-speaking Caribbean will be the main focus of this work. These include, in alphabetical order, Anguilla, Antigua and Barbuda, the Bahamas, Barbados, Belize, Bermuda, British Virgin Islands, Cayman Islands, Commonwealth of Dominica, Grenada, Guyana, Jamaica, Montserrat, St. Kitts and Nevis, St. Lucia, St. Vincent and the Grenadines, Trinidad and Tobago, and the Turks and Caicos Islands. Chapter 1 describes the unique geography and history of these countries and territories, their current political status, and how this impacts their governance and laws. Other chapters focus on foreign, comparative, and international law, the treaty-making process, and emerging legal topics. The authors acknowledge that websites often change, and the links provided at the time of publication were checked and are working.

References

Antoine, Rose-Marie Belle. *Commonwealth Caribbean Law and Legal Systems*. New York: Routledge-Cavendish, 2015.

Newton, Velma. *Commonwealth Caribbean Legal Literature: A Bibliography of All Primary Sources to Date and Secondary Sources for 1971–85*. Cave Hill: Faculty of Law, University of the West Indies, 1987.

Newton, Velma. *Commonwealth Caribbean Legal Systems: A Study of Small Jurisdictions*. Cave Hill: Faculty of Law, University of the West Indies, 1989.

Newton, Velma. *Information Needs and Research Practices of the Commonwealth Caribbean Legal Profession: Report of a Survey Conducted in Six Territories*. Cave Hill: Faculty of Law, University of the West Indies, 1981.

Newton, Velma. *Legal Literature and Conditions Affecting Legal Publishing in the Commonwealth Caribbean: A Bibliography*. Cave Hill: Faculty of Law, University of the West Indies, 1979.

Patchett, Keith, and Jenkins, Valerie. *A Bibliographical Guide to Law in the Commonwealth Caribbean*. Mona: Institute of Social and Economic Research, University of the West Indies, 1973.

Theodore, Michael. *Law: The Air We Breathe: A Look at Law and the Legal System in the Commonwealth Caribbean*. San Juan: Caribbean Legal Publications Ltd., 1994.

Legal Research Methods for the English-Speaking Caribbean

Chapter 1

Caribbean Legal Education: An Overview

Preindependence Caribbean Legal Education

In 1948, a few decades before many countries in the English-speaking Caribbean received their independence from Great Britain, the University of the West Indies (UWI) was established as a branch of the University of London. Its first campus was in Mona, Jamaica. The second campus, in St. Augustine, Trinidad and Tobago, was established in 1960 and evolved from its first faculty, the Imperial College of Tropical Agriculture. In 1962, the UWI became an autonomous institution. A third campus, Cave Hill in Barbados, emerged from a College of Arts in 1963. Meanwhile, tertiary education in the region was bolstered by the establishment of the University of Guyana in October 1963.

Despite the establishment of the UWI as far back as the late 1940s, there was no immediate avenue for the study of law in the Caribbean, and the development of a formal legal education system took a while. Prior to the 1970s, Caribbean nationals interested in studying law, and who had the financial means to do so, would have to travel to the United Kingdom and become a member of one of the four Inns of Court (Inner Temple, Middle Temple, Gray's Inn, and Lincoln's Inn). This was a requirement to fulfill the practical barrister training. Legal training in the United Kingdom operates on a two-track system whereby barristers perform an advocacy role in the courts, and solicitors undertake legal work outside of the courtroom.

Caribbean nationals who could not afford to study abroad would receive legal training through articleships with local attorneys, after which they would take examinations offered by the English Law Society, and then read for the English bar. There was no formal requirement for the completion of a law degree. The prohibitive cost of obtaining legal training outside of the Caribbean meant that only a selective group from the region could pursue a career in law. This also meant that, for a while, there was no room for an organic development of Caribbean law required to address the emerging postindependence legal needs of the region.

Postindependence Legal Education and the Emergence of a Caribbean Model of Education and Practice

The Faculty of Law was established at the Cave Hill campus of the UWI. On September 30, 1971, the treaty establishing the Council of Legal Education (CLE) was ratified; this empowered the CLE to oversee, among other areas, the practical training of Caribbean lawyers (Agreement Establishing the Council of Legal Education, https://www.clecaribbean.com/treaty.php, accessed August 4, 2023). In 1973, the CLE established both the Norman Manley Law School in Jamaica and the Hugh Wooding Law School in Trinidad and Tobago, with a focus on preparing students to practice law.

Formal Caribbean legal education, therefore, evolved in the 1970s into a two-step process of legal studies whereby the academic foundation is laid by the completion of the bachelor of laws (LLB) degree. This is followed by two years of practical training offered at either the Norman Manley Law School in Jamaica or the Hugh Wooding Law School in Trinidad and Tobago, culminating in the CLE's award of the certificate in legal education, which allows the practice of law in the English-speaking Caribbean.

As part of the academic component of this program, students had the option of pursuing the three-year LLB program at the UWI Cave Hill campus. The Council also approved the offering of the first year of the LLB program at the Mona and St. Augustine campuses. The University of Guyana also began offering the LLB program along the line.

A third law school, the Eugene Dupuch Law School, was established in the Bahamas in 1998 to prepare students for the legal education certificate. For foreign nationals who have completed law degrees outside the Caribbean and would like to practice law in the Caribbean, there is a requirement to complete a six-month program at Caribbean law schools. The legal education certificate is awarded after completion of this training and is recognized and accepted in the region as qualification for admission to practice. Figure 1 illustrates the current model of Caribbean legal education.

In 1980, a committee was set up to review the Caribbean legal education system, resulting in the publication of the *Marshall Report*. The committee's work provided an update on the progress and status of Caribbean legal institutions, and made recommendations in the areas of curriculum development and teaching methodologies.

Over time, with growing demand in the region, newer institutions, such as the Truman Bodden Law School in the Cayman Islands (1982) and the University of Technology (2008) in Jamaica, began offering the LLB program. In September 2000, The College of the Bahamas (COB, now University of the Bahamas) imple-

Figure 1 Caribbean Legal Education Process

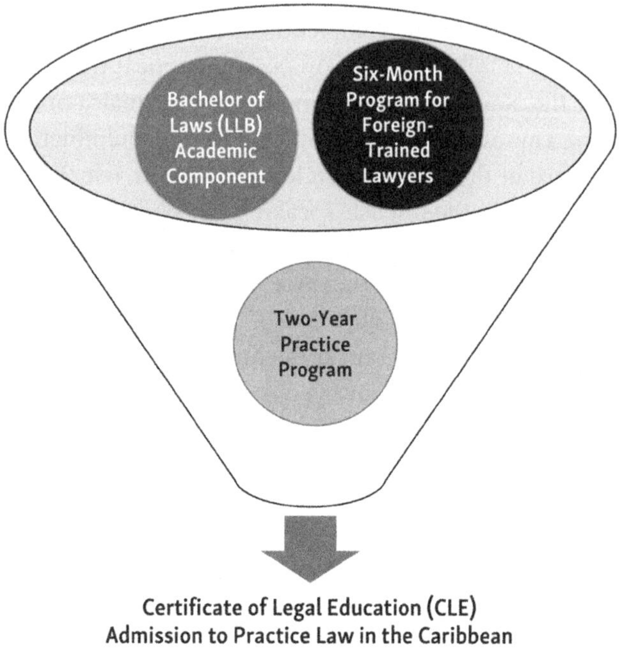

mented its memorandum of understanding with the Faculty of Law, University of the West Indies, Cave Hill to start a joint LLB program. The UWI/COB LLB program became one of the only programs where students could complete their legal training in one place. The newest player in this field is the University of the Commonwealth Caribbean, which now offers the LLB program as an affiliate of the University of London. The program is unique as it is offered online and the degree is awarded by the University of London. This option provides for self-paced or managed learning.

These newer programs have somewhat alleviated the issue of access to legal education in the region. However, there are still only the original three institutions that provide the final phase of training for the legal education certificate, so there are even more students competing for spaces at these institutions.

In 1996, the CLE's Review Committee on Legal Education produced the *Barnett Report*. This report was more in-depth than the earlier *Marshall Report*, and addressed a number of issues, such as:

- expanding capacity to meet the demand for spaces at the three main law schools providing the practice component;
- curriculum review and revision;
- review and revision of admission requirements and the examination system;
- extension of the six-month course for foreign nationals to one year;
- enhancing the law clinic experience for students;
- review and revision of the zoning and quota systems;
- improvement of library facilities to increase study spaces; and
- faculty professional development, publication, recruitment, retention, and pension system.

Legal education has evolved to pursuing advanced degrees in law by citizens of the various Caribbean countries. Specialized master's in law (LLM) programs are now being offered in the region. These include legislative drafting, intellectual property, corporate and commercial law, and public law (UWI, Cave Hill campus), and corporate and commercial law, public law, intellectual property in creative and cultural industries, and the master's in philosophy in law (UWI, Mona campus).

The Status of Caribbean Legal Education in the Twenty-First Century

While there has been significant progress in the training of Caribbean nationals to enter the legal profession, some of the *Barnett Report*'s findings continue to prove challenging. These include the quota and zoning system, the need for more legal clinics and clinical experience, technological and spatial challenges with respect to library services, and the inability of the current three law schools to absorb students who would like to complete the practice component leading to the award of the certificate of legal education.

The Government of Canada is funding an eight-year regional justice sector reform project, entitled Improved Access to Justice in the Caribbean (IMPACT Justice). The Caribbean Law Institute Centre at the Faculty of Law, Cave Hill campus, is implementing the project. According to the Faculty of Law's website, the project's outcome is "enhanced access to justice benefitting men, women, youth and businesses in 13 CARICOM Member States" (Faculty of Law, Cave Hill campus website, https://www.cavehill.uwi.edu/Law/about-us/centres.aspx, accessed August 2, 2023).

By the end of March 2019, one of the completed components of the project was a "region-wide legal education survey to provide governments with information which can be used to shape policy" (Faculty of Law, Cave Hill Campus website, https://www.cavehill.uwi.edu/Law/about-us/centres.aspx, accessed August 2, 2023). A final report from this survey was published in 2017 and outlined several recommendations, including the establishment of additional law schools, in Guyana and two other Caribbean states, to ease the pressure on the current three law schools.

On September 9, 2018, the *Guyana Chronicle* further discussed the issue of quota, spacing, and the need for additional law schools (https://guyanachronicle.com/2018/09/09/owning-a-law-school/, accessed August 2, 2023). Going forward, the issue of clearing the pathway to practice will need to be addressed, given the proliferation of new LLB programs in the region, particularly the online option offered through the University of London, in collaboration with the University of the Commonwealth Caribbean. Also to be considered is the ongoing interest from foreign-trained lawyers for spots in the six-month program.

Clinical Programs

All three law schools currently provide clinical experience for their students in the second year of the program. The number of clinics vary by schools, but mostly align with the economic and social needs of the territories served by the schools. The following is an overview of the current clinic offerings.

Eugene Dupuch Law School Clinics

The Eugene Dupuch Law School currently operates four specialist clinics. Below are details on each of these clinics.

- Commercial and Financial Services Law Clinic: https://eugenedupuchlaw.edu.bs/specialtist-clinics/#1575995869208-f7b4a517-2fcc (accessed August 7, 2023). This clinic has a trust law moot as part of a partnership with STEP (Society of Trust and Estate Practitioners) in the Bahamas.
- Criminal Law Clinic: https://eugenedupuchlaw.edu.bs/specialtist-clinics/#1575995869231-ba40ac72-bbfc (accessed August 7, 2023). One key component of this clinic is the opportunity for students to gain an understanding of the impact of technology, specifically on crime detection and evidence. Students also get firsthand experience on using technology to enhance access to the criminal justice system.
- Environmental Law Clinic: https://eugenedupuchlaw.edu.bs/specialtist-clinics/#1575995880320-104db4a9-5e2c (accessed August 7, 2023). The primary goal of this clinic is "to protect, preserve and conserve the vulnerable resources and environment of The Bahamas" (clinic website, accessed August 7, 2023). Students in this clinic help raise public awareness, and they review current laws and policies and propose amendments to existing legislation and environmental policies. They further hone their legal

research and writing skills by assisting with the annual *Country Report*.

- Human Rights Law Clinic: https://eugenedupuchlaw.edu.bs/specialtist-clinics/#1575995887575-df144bd9-d451 (accessed August 7, 2023). Students in this clinic gain experience in human rights advocacy by working in the community. Some issues that they have focused on include access to housing and clean water. There is also focus on improving legal research and writing skills as well as public education and public speaking.

Hugh Wooding Law School Clinics

The Hugh Wooding Law School has seven clinics listed on its website: https://hwls.edu.tt/courses/legal-aid-clinic/ (accessed August 7, 2023). Unlike the Eugene Dupuch Law School website, which provides access to the description of their clinics, access to the content of the clinics at Hugh Wooding Law School was restricted. However, from the main page of the law school's website, the following clinics were listed:

- Criminal law
- Corporate law
- Human rights
- Oil and gas
- Intellectual property
- Child advocacy
- Environmental law

Norman Manley Law School Clinic

The Norman Manley Law School operates one main Legal Aid Clinic in its provision of practical training (https://nmls.edu.jm/about-clinic, accessed August 7, 2023).

With respect to the services provided, the clinic "accepts general legal matters in addition to cases that fall within the jurisdiction of the Supreme Court, Corporate Area Parish Courts or the Portmore Family Court" (https://nmls.edu.jm/what-we-do, accessed August 7, 2023).

Legal Research Curriculum

The following legal research courses were all identified in the curriculum of the various LLB programs reviewed for this publication:

- Legal methods
- Legal skills
- Legal research and writing
- Research writing
- Academic writing
- Law and legal systems

The expansion of the curriculum indicates that there is ongoing review of Caribbean legal education that will address any gaps and the dated quota and zoning system. The recommendations from these recent reviews will hopefully be acted on by Caribbean governments, especially the need for additional law schools throughout the region, so that the practice component can be completed.

The emergence of online and distance learning options are also helpful for Caribbean nationals who need to balance work and study, or who prefer a more self-paced option, as well as for persons who are unable to gain acceptance at the other institutions offering the LLB program.

References

Note: The selected references below include memoirs and biographies of Caribbean jurists, some of whom played important roles in the establishment of Caribbean legal institutions or legal education. These firsthand accounts are useful for understanding the transition from colonial systems of legal education to the current Caribbean realities.

Anderson, Winston, and Rajnauth-Lee, Maureen, Eds. *Pioneering Caribbean Women Jurists*. Port of Spain: The CCJ Academy for Law, 2021.

Barker, Myrtle. *The Changing Role of the Lawyer in Contemporary Society and its Applicability in the Guyana Context*. Cave Hill: University of the West Indies, 1973.

Barnett, Lloyd. *Report of the Review Committee on Legal Education in the Caribbean. The Barnett Report*. Kingston: Council of Legal Education, 1996.

Biholar, Ramona, Hutchinson, Andrew, and Robinson, Tracy, Eds. *MonaLaw: Revitalising Caribbean Development*. Kingston: Xpress Litho, 2018.

Castagne, Michael R. *Legal Education and the West Indian Lawyer: Past Present and Future. Ontario*. [Self-published], 1976.

Council of Legal Education. *15th Anniversary: Hugh Wooding Law School, 1973–1988*. St. Augustine: University of the West Indies, 1988.

Council of Legal Education. *Professional Law Schools: Regulations*. Mona: Norman Manley Law School, 2000.

Council of Legal Education. *Report of the Review Committee on Legal Education in the Caribbean*. Mona: Council of Legal Education, 1996.

Council of Legal Education. *Report on the Workshop on Legal Education in the Caribbean Held in St. Kitts, April 10–12, 1977*. University of the West Indies, 1977.

Council of Legal Education. Treaty Establishing the Council of Legal Education. https://www.clecaribbean.com/treaty.php (accessed August 4, 2023).

Dina, Yemisi. "Law Libraries in the Bahamas." *Legal Information Management* 2, no. 4 (Winter, 2002): 23–25. https://heinonline.org/HOL/P?h=hein.journals/leginfom2&i=242.

Government of Canada. *Improved Access to Justice in the Caribbean (IMPACT Justice). Report on Survey of Legal Education in CARICOM Member States.* 2017. http://caribbeanimpact.org/website/wp-content/uploads/2021/05/Legal-Education-Survey-Preliminaries.pdf (accessed August 2, 2023).

Guyana Chronicle. "Owning a Law School." September 9, 2018. https://guyanachronicle.com/2018/09/09/owning-a-law-school/ (accessed August 2, 2023).

Hunte, Lewis Stephenson. *Memoirs of a Caribbean Lawyer: The Autobiography of Lewis Stephenson Hunte.* [place of publication unknown]: BookBaby, 2018.

The Marshall Committee. *The Marshall Report.* 1981.

McCalla, Winston C. W. *Legal Aid Developments in the Caribbean.* Miami: University of Miami School of Law, 1980.

Nunez-Tesheira, Karen. *The Legal Profession in the English-Speaking Caribbean.* Kingston: The Caribbean Law Publishing Company, 2001.

Ramjeet, Oscar, Ed. *Training Lawyers in the Caribbean for 50 Years. 1971–2021.* Kingston: Council of Legal Education, 2022.

Ranston, Jackie, and Ranston, Dennis. *Lawyer Manley.* Kingston: University of the West Indies Press, 1998.

Rowe, David P. *Ira Rowe: Caribbean Lawyer: Materials, Tributes and Cases.* Lauderhill: Garai Books, 2006.

Sobion, Justin. *The West Indian Lawyer: Keith Sobion.* Kingston: Council of Legal Education, Research Publications and Legal Education Unit, 2019. (This is a biography of Keith Sobion, former principal of the Norman Manley Law School. He also played an important role in regional integration, including establishment of the Caribbean Court of Justice.)

Wooding, Hugh. *Law in the West Indies: Some Recent Trends*. London: British Institute of International and Comparative Law, 1966. (This work provides important historical information on the development of Caribbean law.)

Chapter 2

The Research Process

Legal research is one of the universal competencies of the legal profession in many jurisdictions. These skills, which are taught and learned in law schools, form the foundation for a successful career in practice.

A competent researcher must be able to:

- locate the relevant statutes or regulation;
- identify the relevant and current cases;
- understand the court structure;
- understand how to use the sources—print or electronic; and
- distinguish between official and unofficial sources.

The research process involves identifying and understanding the appropriate resources you need to consult when conducting legal research.

It involves finding current and accurate information. This is very important in the digital age where information is freely available from various sources. Many government websites provide free access to statutes, regulation, legislative materials, and case law. Others can be found on subscription and fee-based databases, some of which have been identified in this book.

Bhat (2020, p. 11) defines the legal research process as: "Identifying the most appropriate law, determining questions of fact for the application of law. . . ." He further breaks down legal research into analytical, historical, philosophical, and comparative methods.

This concept should be applied when working on Caribbean legal research. It is critical for you to identify the kind of materials you will need for your work. It is important to understand where you can locate primary and secondary sources of law. Knowing and understanding where to start will save you time.

A fundamental knowledge of the history of the Caribbean jurisdiction you are researching is of great importance. For example, you need to understand whether the country is an independent one or an Overseas Territory. This book covers the English-speaking Caribbean countries, many of which have historical ties to the United Kingdom as former British colonies. Because of the historical relationship between these countries, there are several commonalities in their legal literature; the content and names of their legislation are similar. For example, in the Caribbean, there is the Companies Act of Jamaica like the Companies Act of the United Kingdom. These facts are all relevant to the research process when identifying the legal materials of these jurisdictions.

Secondary sources of law provide a broader understanding about a topic or jurisdiction. They include books, journal articles, blogs, finding tools, etc. Table 1 provides a listing of secondary resources with examples.

As a rule, always start your research with a secondary source. For example, if you are writing a paper on immigration in the Caribbean, one of the first research steps would be writing out your research questions and how you plan to answer them. As a first step, you want to limit the focus of this paper to one or two Caribbean nations. Next you want to find information on the immigration law of the selected jurisdiction. After identifying the countries, you want to find out whether that jurisdiction is an independent one or British Overseas Territory.

Table 1 Secondary Sources

Secondary Source	Information	Example
Books/ treatises	A book is written by a specialist on a subject. It describes and gives you a broader understanding of the subject with examples, case law, and legislation.	1. Commonwealth Caribbean law and legal systems 2. Commonwealth Caribbean tort law 3. Commonwealth Caribbean sports law
Journals	Articles are written by experts and published in different journals. It could be the outcome of a study or research by the author. Articles focusing on the Caribbean can be found in many journals published in the United Kingdom, Canada, Australia, and the United States.	1. *Caribbean Law Review* 2. *Common World Law Review* 3. *Jamaica Law Journal*
Encyclopedias	An encyclopedia describes the different legal concepts using case law, legislation and legal instruments. While there are no specific legal encyclopedias for the Caribbean, legal researchers can use any UK legal encyclopedia.	1. *Halsbury's Laws of England* 2. *Encyclopedia of Forms & Precedents*
Current awareness and finding tools	A finding tool helps locate all relevant legal information about a jurisdiction. This is very useful when researching about foreign jurisdictions, especially non-English-speaking ones.	1. Globalex: Foreign Law Research (https://www.nyulawglobal.org/globalex/) 2. Foreign Law Guide

Digests/ abridgements	Digests are used to identify case law on different legal topics. They explain how the courts have used a point in determining a case. There has been no digests or abridgements published and originating from the Caribbean. Legal researchers tend to rely on other digests from the United Kingdom because of the similarity and dependence on the common law.	1. *The Digest: Annotated British, Commonwealth and European Cases* 2. *Current Law Yearbook*
Indexes	Indexes provide a summary of the full volume of a work published. They can be found at the end of a book where you will find the page number reference. The indexes in this context reference journal articles or legislation. Indexes for journal articles sometimes provide access to the full text of the journal as in the case of *LegalTrac*, which is an online database. The *Consolidated Index of Statutes and Subsidiary Legislation* is exclusively in print.	1. *Consolidated Index of Statutes and Subsidiary Legislation* 2. *Index to Foreign Legal Periodicals* 3. *LegalTrac*
Dictionaries	Dictionaries provide the definition of legal terms. They are different from the conventional dictionary. Definitions found in them include Latin phrases that are found in legal language. Many jurisdictions have their own dictionaries, but there is none yet for the Caribbean. Legal researchers rely on legal dictionaries published in the United Kingdom.	1. *Words and phrases legally defined* 2. *Osborn's concise law dictionary* 3. *Jowitt's dictionary of English law* 4. *Stroud's judicial dictionary of English law*

Citators	This publication provides the full meaning and abbreviations for many law reports and journals. Legal practitioners rely on United Kingdom sources as there are none originating from the Caribbean. Technology has simplified the access to this database, which is now available online.	1. Cardiff index to legal abbreviations (https://www.legalabbrevs.cardiff.ac.uk/)
Bibliographies	Bibliographies list sources of legal information such as articles, books, and legislation. Some bibliographies are topical or cover different jurisdictions or institutions in the region.	1. *Commonwealth Caribbean legal literature: A bibliography of all primary sources to date and secondary sources for 1971–1985* 2. *Women and the law: A bibliographical survey of legal and quasi-legal materials with special reference to Commonwealth Caribbean jurisdictions and including relevant Commonwealth Caribbean legislation and case material*
Research guides	Research guides are tools prepared by librarians to assist users to find resources available to them on different topics. The current practice in many academic libraries is to publish these guides on the Springshare platform LibGuides.	Caribbean: legal resources (Bodleian Law Library, Oxford University)

Blogs	These are independent write-ups on different legal topics.	1. Caribbean Law (https://caribbeanlaw2019.com/blog/) 2. Caribbean Trade Law and Development (https://caribbeantradelaw.com/2019/04/02/ctld-blog-rated-among-top-30-caribbean-blogs-to-follow-in-2019/)

A good strategy is to identify what you are looking for—a book, bibliography, case law, statute, or journal article. It is important to identify whether the information is available in print or online.

An important competency for legal research as earlier mentioned is the ability to understand and identify the appropriate resources and where to locate them. The collection of the Faculty of Law Library, University of the West Indies Cave Hill, Barbados is one of the largest and most extensive in the region. The library's online catalogue can be searched globally. Additionally, researchers can always search the collection of other libraries in the region on WorldCat.

As the world continues to embrace artificial intelligence, it is important to emphasize that the research process involves carefully checking all materials and their sources. Caution should be exercised and researchers should not rely solely on machine learning models' predictions when conducting legal research about the Caribbean. It is important to note that some materials from this region are still predominantly in print, and having an expectation to get answers from tools like ChatGPT will be a futile exercise.

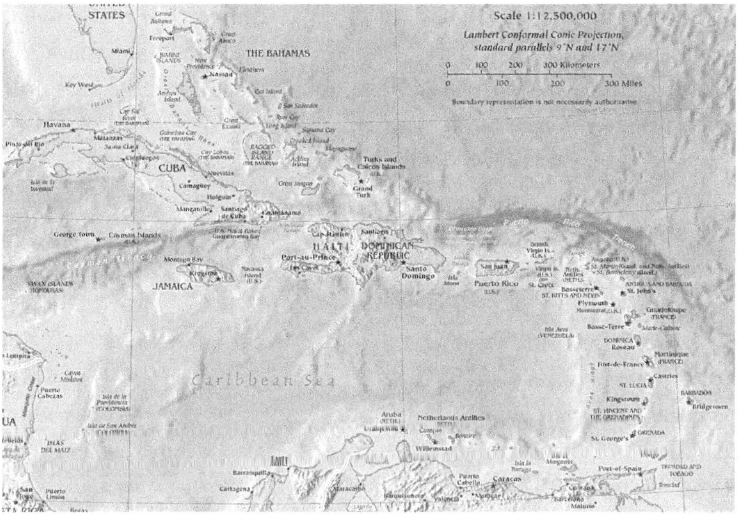

Figure 2 CIA map of the Caribbean

Source: CIA World Factbook, https://commons.wikimedia.org/wiki/File:CIA_map_of_the_Caribbean.png (accessed August 9, 2023).

The Geography, History, and Politics of the English-Speaking Caribbean States

The Caribbean Sea is located on the borders of many islands that are English, French, Spanish, and Dutch speaking. The larger islands such as Cuba, Jamaica, Puerto Rico, Haiti, and the Dominican Republic are called the Greater Antilles, while the smaller islands in the eastern Caribbean are called the Lesser Antilles. The countries covered in this work, despite being geographically dispersed, have a shared history as English-speaking former colonies of Great Britain. As a result of this history, both their political structures and legal systems have been influenced by the Westminster model of government and the English common law.

Some of these island nations in the Caribbean basin are twin-islands or archipelagic states. Jamaica and the Cayman Islands are located in the western Caribbean, the British Virgin Islands in the central Caribbean, while the Bahamas and Turks and Caicos Islands are located in the northeast. Anguilla, Antigua and Barbuda, Barbados, Commonwealth of Dominica, Grenada, St. Kitts and Nevis, St. Lucia, St. Vincent and the Grenadines, and Trinidad and Tobago are all located in the eastern Caribbean. A further distinction among the eastern Caribbean islands relates to the division between the Windward and Leeward islands. The location of the Windward Islands such as St. Lucia, Grenada, and others place them in the path of prevailing trade winds. The Leeward Islands are made up of the more northerly and sheltered islands like Anguilla and Antigua and Barbuda.

Belize, Bermuda, and Guyana all have interesting geography. Belize, though west of the Caribbean Sea, is actually in Central America, south of the Yucatán Peninsula, and shares its northern border with Mexico and is located east of Guatemala. Guyana lies on the northeastern edge of South America, and its neighbors are Venezuela, Brazil, and Suriname. Bermuda is in the North Atlantic Ocean, approximately 650 miles east of Cape Hatteras, North Carolina.

Long the pawns in British, French, Spanish, Dutch, and Danish hegemonic struggles, these territories having endured slavery and colonization, and they emerged from rebellions and agitation to finally gain their independence starting around the early 1960s. Their tentative steps toward economic and political collaboration ended in the short-lived West Indies Federation (discussed further in chapter 6). Despite this setback, the pursuit of cooperation continued, meeting eventual success in several enduring initiatives such as the Caribbean Community, Organisation of Eastern Caribbean States, the Caribbean Development Bank, the Caribbean Court of Justice, and several other regional organizations. Four Caribbean states have republic status: Guyana (1970), Trinidad and Tobago (1976), Dominica (1978), and the newest, Barbados (2021).

The Caribbean has not been immune to political upheavals. In the postcolonial period, as the region tried to find its footing as newly independent nations, there were political growing pains, and the Caribbean also became entangled in Cold War machinations. In March 1979, there was the Grenada Revolution, with the proclamation of the People's Revolutionary Government. This ultimately led to the invasion of Grenada by the United States. In Trinidad, there was a coup attempt by the Jamaat al Muslimeen in July 1990. Larger states such as Jamaica and Guyana also did not escape political turmoil, with escalating political violence in those territories throughout the 1970s and beyond. In Jamaica, Guyana, and Grenada, tensions with the United States stemmed from the close relations between these countries and Cuba, and in Jamaica's case, the articulation of democratic socialism as a political path by then leader of the People's National Party, Michael Manley. From as early as 1970, Jamaica, Trinidad and Tobago, and Guyana joined the Non-Aligned Movement. Grenada followed in 1979, and several other English-speaking Caribbean states joined in the mid-1980s and onward. Despite the early teething pains following independence, these states are generally regarded as stable democracies, with several countries in this group ranking highly on the index for press freedom.

With its unique legal, political, and economic circumstances, the English-speaking Caribbean continues to attempt to shape its laws to match Caribbean realities. However, there is still much work to be done to overhaul a legal system that was designed to buttress British hegemony in the region, and with legislative intentions that enhanced racial and economic oppression. There are, therefore, ongoing reforms in a number of areas, so that ultimately, Caribbean law can be relevant for the citizens and their situations and a reflection of twenty-first-century economic and social realities.

Some future considerations are the outcome of the quest for reparations from Britain; whether more Caribbean territories will fully embrace the Caribbean Court of Justice as a court of last resort, thereby letting go of the Judicial Committee of the Privy Council; the direction that the current British Overseas Territories will take in terms of their relationship with the United Kingdom; and the impact of court and legislative reforms on social justice, sentencing, and economic equity.

References

Note: Although the following titles are not specific to the Caribbean, they nevertheless provide a thorough understanding of the legal research process. They are also useful for researching the laws of other jurisdictions beyond the Caribbean.

Allbon, Emily, and Dua, Sanmeet Kaur. *The Insider's Guide to Legal Skills*. Abingdon: Routledge, 2023.

Ballin, Ernst Hirsch. *Advanced Introduction to Legal Research Methods*. Cheltenham: Edward Elgar Publishing Limited, 2020.

Barkan, Steven M., Bintliff, Barbara, and Whisner, Mary. *Fundamentals of Legal Research*. St. Paul: Foundation Press, 2015.

Bhat, Ishwara P. *Ideas and Methods of Legal Research*. New Delhi: Oxford University Press, 2020.

Clinch, Peter. *Legal Research: A Practitioner's Handbook*. London: Wildy, Simmonds and Hill Publishing, 2013.

Deplano, Rossana, and Tsagourias, Nikolaos, Eds. *Research Methods in International Law: A Handbook*. Cheltenham: Edward Elgar Publishing Limited, 2021.

Knowles, John, and Thomas, Philip A. *Effective Legal Research*, 4th ed. London: Sweet and Maxwell, 2016.

Kunz, Christina L. *The Process of Legal Research*. 7th ed. New York: Aspen Publishers, 2008.

Olson, Kent. *Legal Research in a Nutshell*. 13th ed. St. Paul: West Academic, 2018.

Putman, William H., and Albright, Jennifer. *Legal Research.* Stamford: Cengage Learning, 2016.

Sloan, Amy E. *Basic Legal Research: Tools and Strategies.* New York: Wolters Kluwer, 2012.

Tjaden, Ted. *Legal Research and Writing.* Toronto: Irwin Law, 2016.

Chapter 3

Researching Caribbean Constitutions

Definition of Constitutions

Constitutions have been described as the "supreme law," dynamic and growing instruments. They are sacred and keep evolving. The Caribbean constitutions each have unique historical contexts that will guide the understanding of the legal systems of each country. Researching the Caribbean constitutions requires an in-depth knowledge of the historical developments in the region. There have been different stages of constitutional developments in the region that have emerged from colonial days to date.

When researching constitutions, it is important to distinguish between the independent countries (Jamaica, Trinidad and Tobago, Guyana, Barbados, the Bahamas, Grenada, Dominica, St. Lucia, St. Vincent and the Grenadines, Belize, Antigua and Barbuda, and St. Kitts and Nevis) and the British Overseas Territories (Anguilla, British Virgin Islands, the Cayman Islands, and the Turks and Caicos Islands). The constitutions of the Overseas Territories can be found in Orders in Council.

Many of the constitutions of these countries are available online on the government websites. They can be also accessed in the following subscription databases:

- HeinOnline's World Constitutions Illustrated: The World Constitutions database has over 120 constitutions with those of 12 independent English-speaking Caribbean countries. This database includes historical and current constitutions.
- Oxford Constitutions of the World: This database contains historical and current materials from independent countries and the British Overseas Territories. The database features Constitutional Overviews, Constitution Orders, Constitutional Amendment Orders, and Reports of Constitutional Conferences.
- LLMC Digital (historical constitutions): This database provides access to historical constitutions; LLMC Digital has a selection of Constitutional Conference Reports from all over the region. These materials contain detailed reports and agreements.
- The Constitute Project (https://www.constituteproject.org/, accessed May 24, 2022, and July 22, 2023) also provides links to the world's constitutions with recent amendments. This database covers thirteen countries from the English-speaking Caribbean.

Below are links to constitutions and constitutional resources of English-speaking Caribbean nations that are available on the internet:

- Anguilla: https://www.legislation.gov.uk/uksi/1982/334/made (accessed May 24, 2022, and July 22, 2023)
- Antigua and Barbuda: https://pdba.georgetown.edu/Constitutions/Antigua/antigua-barbuda.html (accessed May 30, 2022, and July 22, 2023)

- The Bahamas: https://bit.ly/3obngLf (accessed May 24, 2022, and July 22, 2023)
- Barbados: https://www.oas.org/dil/the_constitution_of_barbados.pdf (accessed May 30, 2022, and July 22, 2023). Note: Barbados recently amended its Constitution (Amendment (No. 2) Bill 2021). The purpose of the amendment is to allow Barbados to become a republic with a president as the head of state. https://www.barbadosparliament.com/uploads/bill_resolution/56f53e308108b4b315d1b367c2914f7a.pdf
- Belize: https://www.agm.gov.bz/uploads/laws/63bdc04dbf895_Cap_04_Belize_Constitution_Act.pdf (accessed May 10, 2022, and July 22, 2023)
- Bermuda: https://guides.loc.gov/law-bermuda/constitution (accessed May 30, 2022, and July 22, 2023)
- British Virgin Islands: https://bvi.gov.vg/sites/default/files/constitution.pdf (accessed May 30, 2022, and July 22, 2023)
- Cayman Islands: https://legislation.gov.ky/cms/legislation/constitution/current.html (accessed May 30, 2022, and July 22, 2023)
- Dominica: https://www.constituteproject.org/constitution/Dominica_2014?lang=en(accessed May 30, 2022, and July 22, 2023)
- Grenada: https://www.constituteproject.org/constitution/Grenada_1992?lang=en (accessed May 30, 2022, and July 22, 2023)
- Guyana: https://www.constituteproject.org/constitution/Guyana_2016.pdf?lang=en (accessed May 30, 2022, and July 22, 2023)
- Jamaica: https://www.constituteproject.org/constitution/Jamaica_2015?lang=en (accessed May 30, 2022, and July 22, 2023)

- Montserrat: https://www.gov.ms/wp-content/uploads/2020/06/MNI-Constitution-Order-Oct-2010.pdf (accessed September 20, 2023)
- St. Kitts and Nevis: https://www.constituteproject.org/constitution/St_Kitts_and_Nevis_1983?lang=en (accessed May 30, 2022, and July 22, 2023)
- St. Lucia: https://www.constituteproject.org/constitution/St_Lucia_1978?lang=en (accessed May 30, 2022, and July 22, 2023)
- St. Vincent and the Grenadines: https://www.constituteproject.org/constitutions?lang=en&status=in_force&status=is_draft (accessed May 30, 2022, and July 22, 2023)
- Trinidad and Tobago: https://www.constituteproject.org/constitution/Trinidad_and_Tobago_2007?lang=en (accessed May 30, 2022, and July 22, 2023)
- Turks and Caicos Islands: https://www.legislation.gov.uk/uksi/2011/1681/contents/made (accessed May 30, 2022, and July 22, 2023)

References

Albert, Richard, O'Brien, Derek, and Seshauna, Wheatle. *The Oxford Handbook of Caribbean Constitutions*. Oxford: Oxford University Press, 2020.

Alexis, Francis. *Changing Caribbean Constitutions*, 2nd ed. Christ Church: Carib Research and Publications, 2015.

Batts, David. *The Law and Constitution for Every Jamaican*. Kingston: The Caribbean Law Publishing Company, 2022.

Berry, David S., and Robinson, Tracy S. *Transitions in Caribbean Law: Law Making, Constitutionalism, and the Convergence of National and International Law*. Kingston: The Caribbean Law Publishing Company, 2013.

Dupont, Jerry. *The Common Law Abroad: Constitutional and Legal Legacy of the British Empire.* Littleton: F. B. Rothman Publications, 2001. (This is also available as an e-book.)

Ghany, Hamid A. *Constitutional Development in the Commonwealth Caribbean.* Kingston: Ian Randle Publishers, 2018.

McIntosh, Simeon C.R. *Fundamental Rights and Democratic Governance: Essays in Caribbean Jurisprudence.* Kingston: Caribbean Law Publishing, 2005.

Meeks, Brian, and Quinn, Kate, Eds. *Beyond Westminster in the Caribbean.* Kingston: Ian Randle Publishers, 2018.

O'Brien, Derek. *The Constitutional Systems of the Commonwealth Caribbean: A Contextual Analysis.* Oxford: Hart Publishing, 2014.

Phillips, Fred. *Commonwealth Caribbean Constitutional Law.* London. Routledge-Cavendish, 2016.

Robinson, Tracy S., Bulkan, Arif, and Saunders, Adrian. *Fundamentals of Caribbean Constitutional Law.* London: Sweet and Maxwell, 2021.

Chapter 4

Researching Legislation: Statutes and Regulations

The legislation of Caribbean jurisdictions can be found in statutes and regulations passed by lawmakers in Parliament. These materials are predominantly available in print, and are published by government printers of each jurisdiction and in some instances by commercial publishers. The Caribbean Community Secretariat (CARICOM) has published some model legislation; see a full list in the references.

The advancement of technology has created immediate access to legislation from selected jurisdictions on the internet. For citation purposes, some jurisdictions recognize the electronic versions of legislations as official publications. It is important to check whether the materials available online have been recognized as official publications before citing them.

Government Publishers

The following countries have made their legislation available on the internet:

- Anguilla: http://www.gov.ai/laws.php (accessed May 26, 2022, and July 31, 2023)
  Coverage: 2014 revised laws of Anguilla in force as of December 14, 2014; 1856–2014 multilateral treaties; United Kingdom statutory instruments, local statutory instruments, conventions, and multilateral treaties applicable to Anguilla.
- Antigua and Barbuda: http://laws.gov.ag/# (accessed May 26, 2022, and July 31, 2023)
  Coverage: Selected bills; statutory instruments, 1993–2022; annuals, 1993–2023; laws of Antigua and Barbuda, revised edition, 1992, Volumes 1–9; and selected repealed laws and subsidiary legislation, Volumes 10–15.
- The Bahamas: https://laws.bahamas.gov.bs/cms/legislation.html (accessed May 26, 2022, and July 31, 2023)
  Coverage: Acts, subsidiary legislation, repealed laws, and index (1920–2023).
- Barbados: https://gisbarbados.gov.bb/the-official-gazette/ (accessed May 26, 2022, and July 2023)
  Coverage: This is the website of the Barbados Government Information Services providing access to the *Official Gazette* and selected statutory instruments from July 2018.
- Belize: https://www.agm.gov.bz/laws/ (accessed May 26, 2022, and July 31, 2023)
  Coverage: Indices; substantive laws, Volumes 1–18; acts, 2021–2023; and subsidiary laws.
- Bermuda: http://www.bermudalaws.bm/SitePages/Home.aspx (accessed May 26, 2022, and July 31, 2023)
  Coverage: Annual laws, consolidated laws, laws not in force, repealed/revoked laws, annual laws index.
- British Virgin Islands:
  - Coverage: This website provides access to selected legislation of the British Virgin Islands.

  - The *Official Gazette* is available by subscription (https://eservices.gov.vg/gazette/#:~:text=The%20Gazette%20is%20the%20official,Gazette%20from%20time%20to%20time, acccssed September 20, 2023).
- Cayman Islands: https://legislation.gov.ky/cms/legislation/current.html (accessed May 26, 2022, and August 5, 2023)
  Coverage: The website covers current legislation, repealed/spent acts, revoked secondary legislation, not in force, and index.
- Dominica: http://dominica.gov.dm/laws-of-dominica (accessed May 26, 2022, and August 19, 2023)
  Coverage: The website provides access to the Revised Laws of Dominica 1990, acts and statutory rules, and orders, 1991–2009.
- Guyana: https://officialgazette.gov.gy/index.php/publications (accessed May 26, 2022)
  Coverage: This website provides access to the *Official Gazettes* of Guyana 2013 to 2021.
- Jamaica:
  - Ministry of Justice Jamaica, Acts and Subsidiary Legislation (https://moj.gov.jm/laws, accessed May 26, 2022, and August 19, 2023)
    Coverage: This is the website of the Ministry of Justice. It provides access to the digitized volumes of the Revised Laws of Jamaica, Volumes I–XXVII
  - Jamaica Parliament, Acts from 2009 to 2021 (https://japarliament.gov.jm/index.php, accessed May 26, 2022)
    Coverage: This is the website of the Houses of Parliament. It provides access to acts, bills, order papers, regulations, resolutions, and orders, among others.
- Montserrat: http://agc.gov.ms/?page_id=352 (accessed May 26, 2022, and August 19, 2023)

Coverage: The government website provides access to acts (revised and passed), statutory rules and orders, and statutory instruments, among others.

- St. Kitts and Nevis: https://lawcommission.gov.kn/#gsc.tab=0 (accessed August 19, 2023)
  Coverage: The website of the Law Commission of St. Kitts & Nevis provides access to selected revised acts, annual laws, revised ordinances of Nevis, and repealed acts and ordinances.
- Trinidad and Tobago: http://laws.gov.tt/ (accessed May 26, 2022, and August 19, 2023)
  Coverage: This Digital Legislative Library provides access to the laws of Trinidad and Tobago from 1838 to 2023.
- Turks and Caicos: https://www.gov.tc/agc/laws/annual (accessed May 26, 2022, and August 19, 2023)
  Coverage: The website of the Attorney General's Chambers provides access to revised laws and annual laws (subsidiary legislation and ordinances).

The Law Library, Faculty of Law, University of the West Indies, Cave Hill campus, Barbados publishes the *Consolidated West Indian Legislation Index Project Index* of statutes and subsidiary legislation for countries in the region. This index is a compilation of periodic updates of statutes and subsidiary legislation. This is a very useful tool for updating and noting changes when researching legislation.

Commercial Publishers

- Global Regulation provides access to legislation, including subsidiary legislation of ten English-speaking Caribbean jurisdictions.
- LLMC Digital provides access to historical legislation for all English-speaking Caribbean countries.

- vLex Justis provides access to West Indian law reports and unreported cases compiled by CARILAW, a database of the Faculty of Law, University of the West Indies, Cave Hill, Barbados.
- Other commercial publishers like LexisNexis and Thomson Reuters provide access to selected legislation of some Caribbean jurisdictions.

References

CARICOM Model Legislation on Citizenship. CARICOM Secretariat, 1997.

CARICOM Model Legislation on Domestic Violence. CARICOM Secretariat, 1997.

CARICOM Model Legislation on Equality for Women in Employment. CARICOM Secretariat, 1997.

CARICOM Model Legislation on Equal Pay. CARICOM Secretariat, 1997.

CARICOM Model Legislation on Inheritance. CARICOM Secretariat, 1997.

CARICOM Model Legislation on Maintenance and Maintenance Orders. CARICOM Secretariat, 1997.

CARICOM Model Legislation on Sexual Harassment. CARICOM Secretariat,1997.

CARICOM Model Legislation on Sexual Offences. CARICOM Secretariat, 1997.

Charter of Civil Society for the Caribbean Community. CARICOM Secretariat, 1997.

Horna, Angel V. *Law of the Sea and Maritime Delimitation: State Practice and Case Law in Latin America and the Caribbean*. Abingdon: Routledge, 2023.

Legal Deposit of National Publications: A Report and Model Legislation. CARICOM Secretariat, 1978.

Simmons, David A. C., and Blackman, Christopher, Eds. *The Barbados Employment Rights Tribunal Reports, 2015–2021*. Bridgetown: The Improved Access to Justice in the Caribbean Project (IMPACT Justice), 2023.

Chapter 5

Local Government: Finding Municipal Laws

Municipal laws are enacted at the local level in counties, parishes, or districts. These laws or ordinances cover wide areas of operations such as taxation, zoning, parks, markets, licenses, and environmental issues. Local governance varies across the Caribbean and depends on a variety of factors; for instance, the status of the state (i.e., independent, or overseas territory), size, and the structure of the central government. This latter point on the structure of the central government is important.

Ministerial designations are fluid and often change, particularly after an election. The websites of the various governments are usually the most reliable, current, and authoritative sources to start your research on municipal laws. Most of these websites provide links to approved and pending legislation, reports, other official documents, and press releases. The Law Library of Congress's Guide to Law Online (https://guides.loc.gov/law-library, accessed May 30, 2022) provides comprehensive coverage on the laws of many states, and links to individual country profiles are provided throughout this section. In addition, the Commonwealth Local Government Forum (https://www.clgf.org.uk/regions/clgf-americas/, accessed May 30, 2022) provides extensive country reports on local government in

Commonwealth countries. Where available, links to these reports will also be provided below.

Local government reform has been an important focus for several governments in the region over the past two decades. Development partners such as the Caribbean Development Bank, United Nations Development Program, as well as from other regional and international organizations, have been engaged in this process to further develop local government initiatives.

Many Caribbean states are divided into either districts or parishes, which are equivalent to provinces or states. Government ministries with a focus on local governance normally exercise oversight of municipal corporations. Several jurisdictions do not have specific local government ministries. However, as stated above, this can change over time, depending on future government focus. In addition, some constitutions outline territorial administration, as is the case, for example, in St. Kitts and Nevis, discussed below.

This section will describe the existing municipal and local governance structures throughout the region and review online and print sources for locating municipal laws. A brief bibliography on local government structures and reforms in the region follows the section.

Anguilla

Anguilla is an Overseas Territory of the United Kingdom, with internal self-governance. It has a multiparty system and is divided into fourteen districts. Presently, there is no specific ministry with oversight for local governance. The Government of Anguilla's website (http://gov.ai/index.php, accessed May 30, 2022) has a Document Library (http://gov.ai/document_library.php, accessed May 30, 2022) section. This is where laws and regulations, draft bills, general orders, and executive council minutes are located. The *Official Gazette* (http://gazette.gov.ai/, accessed May 30, 2022) is published monthly on the last day of each month. In addition to Bills and Acts, it also publishes Notices and other official documents.

The following are additional print and online sources for researching Anguilla's municipal laws:

- Anguilla Consolidated Index to Statutes and Subsidiary Legislation. Faculty of Law Cave Hill, University of the West Indies.
- Hendry, I. D., and Dickson, Susan. *British Overseas Territories Law*. Oxford: Hart, 2018. (This book covers the laws of the fourteen remaining British Overseas Territories.)
- *Leeward Islands Gazette*. Antigua Government Printer, 1900–1956.
- Statutory Rules and Orders. TWI, Basseterre, St. Kitts. (Contains Delegated Legislation for Anguilla and St. Kitts and Nevis.)
- Guide to Caribbean Law Research (https://www.nyulawglobal.org/globalex/Caribbean1.html, accessed May 30, 2022).
- Guide to Law Online Anguilla, Law Library of Congress (https://guides.loc.gov/law-anguilla#legal, accessed May 30, 2022).

Antigua and Barbuda

Antigua and Barbuda comprise the six parishes in Antigua, and the two dependent islands of Barbuda and Redonda. There is no specific ministry with a focus on local government. From its Antigua and Barbuda Laws site (http://laws.gov.ag/, accessed May 30, 2022), there are links to Bills (http://laws.gov.ag/bills/), Laws or Acts of Parliaments (http://laws.gov.ag/laws/alphabetical/), and Statutory Instruments (http://laws.gov.ag/statutory/, all accessed May 30, 2022).

The following are additional print and online sources for researching Antigua and Barbuda's laws:

- *Antigua and Barbuda: Consolidated Index of Statutes and Subsidiary Legislation to 1st January 2015*. Faculty of Law, University of the West Indies.
- *Antigua and Barbuda Laws*. Antigua and Barbuda: Government Printer, 1982.
- *The Antigua and Barbuda Official Gazette*. Government Printer, 1981.
- *Eastern Caribbean Law Reports*. Kingston: Caribbean Law Publishing Company, 2003.
- Guide to Law Online: Antigua and Barbuda, Law Library of Congress. https://guides.loc.gov/law-antigua-barbuda (accessed May 30, 2022).
- Jacobs, Wilfred. *Laws of Antigua and Barbuda*. London: Eyre and Spottiswoode.
- *Statutory Instruments, 1981*. Government Printer, 1992.

The Bahamas

Local governance in the archipelagic state of the Bahamas falls under the Department of Lands and Local Government, for which the Office of the Prime Minister has oversight. There are thirty-two local government districts in the Bahamas, and these districts are divided into second-schedule and third-schedule district councils. There are thirteen second-schedule districts and nineteen third-schedule districts. The exception is the island of New Providence, where the capital, Nassau, is located. Its affairs are managed by the central government. New local government areas are formed depending on demographics. Prior to the current system of local government, an appointed Board of Works existed. However, most of the final decisions were made by the central government.

The following are additional print and online sources for researching the laws of the Bahamas:

- Bahamas Laws Online (http://laws.bahamas.gov.bs/cms/en/, accessed May 28, 2022), Office of the Attorney General and Ministry of Legal Affairs. It contains all legislation in force up to December 31, 2009, as well as new and amended legislation in force from January 1, 2010, onward.
- *The Commonwealth of the Bahamas: Consolidated Index of Statutes and Subsidiary Legislation to 1st January, 2015.* Faculty of Law Library, University of the West Indies, 2015.
- Guide to Law Online: Commonwealth of the Bahamas, Law Library of Congress (https://guides.loc.gov/law-bahamas, accessed May 28, 2022).
- *The Subsidiary Legislation of the Bahamas, 1799–2000: In Force on the 2nd of April 2002.* Juta & Co.

Barbados

Barbados, a parliamentary democracy, is divided into eleven parishes. However, it does not have an elected local government. With the passage of the Constituency Council Act of 2009, the Department of Constituency Empowerment was created within the Ministry of Social Care, Constituency Empowerment, and Community Development. This department's mandate is the creation of constituency councils for the thirty constituencies in Barbados.

The following are additional print and online sources for researching the laws of Barbados:

- *Barbados: Consolidated Index of Statutes and Subsidiary Legislation to 1st January 2015.* Faculty of Law Library. Cave Hill: University of the West Indies.
- Goodman, G. Aubrey. 2015 *Laws of Barbados. Revised and Consolidated.* [Place of publication not identified]: Forgotten Books, 2015.

- Guide to Law Online Barbados, Law Library of Congress (https://guides.loc.gov/law-barbados, accessed May 28, 2022).
- *The Laws of Barbados 2015 with Indices: Acts 1–33*. Barbados: Attorney General's Office, 2015.

Belize

The local government structure in Belize comprises seven towns and city municipalities, and these are each governed by a mayor and councillors. Based on the most recent data from the Government of Belize website, local government issues fall under the Ministry of Rural Transformation, Community Development, Labour, and Local Government. The following is a description of local governance:

> Belize has two levels of government: a state government and a single-tier local government. Over the last five years, local councils have been formally established and the trend has been towards greater decentralisation and autonomy.

Village councils mainly cover the rural areas. They hold elections every three years for the positions of council members and chairperson. Community councils are like village councils, but they are formed in areas that are not within a city or village. Community councils require the community to be declared, after which it is accepted based on a ministerial order.

There is a Municipal Court (https://www.belizejudiciary.org/magistracy/municipal-court/, accessed May 30, 2022) administered under the Inferior Court Act. This court hears cases from the Belize City Municipality, and these cases concern business and trade licenses, traffic, property tax, and liquor licenses. The following are some important legislations related to local governance:

- Belize City Council Act 1999
- Belmopan City Council Act 1999

- Inferior Courts Act 2000
- Town Councils Act 1999
- Village Councils Act 1999

The following are additional print and online sources for researching the laws of Belize:

- The Belize Legal Information Network (https://www.belizelaw.org/cgi-sys/suspendedpage.cgi, accessed May 28, 2022) provides access to Local Government (https://www.belizelaw.org/cgi-sys/suspendedpage.cgi, accessed May 28, 2022) legislation under Volume II, Title VIII.
- Guide to Law Online Belize, Law Library of Congress (https://guides.loc.gov/law-belize, accessed May 28, 2022).
- *The Substantive Laws of Belize: In Force on the 31st Day of December 2000*. Government Printer, 2001.

Bermuda

Bermuda does not have a defined government agency for local governance. See the Department and Ministries (https://www.gov.bm/departments-and-ministries#l, accessed May 30, 2022) page for a listing of more details on the structure of government. Bermuda Laws Online (http://www.bermudalaws.bm/SitePages/Home.aspx, accessed May 30, 2022) also provides links to legislation.

The following print and online sources are useful for in-depth Bermuda legal research:

- *Bermuda Consolidated Index of Public Acts and Subsidiary Legislation to 1st January 1996*. Faculty of Law, University of the West Indies.
- *Bermuda Law Reports*. Justis Publishing Ltd., 2002.

- Guide to Law Online Bermuda, Law Library of Congress (https://guides.loc.gov/law-bermuda, accessed May 30, 2022).
- Hendry, I. D., and Dickson, Susan. *British Overseas Territories Law*. Oxford: Hart, 2018. (This publication covers the laws of the fourteen remaining British Overseas Territories.)
- *The Revised Laws of Bermuda*. Bermuda Press Ltd., 1992.

British Virgin Islands

The British Virgin Islands are a British Overseas Territory. There is no designated ministry or department responsible for local governance in the British Virgin Islands.

The following are additional print and online sources for researching the laws of the British Virgin Islands:

- *British Virgin Islands Consolidated Index of Statutes and Subsidiary Legislation to 1st January 2015*. Faculty of Law, University of the West Indies.
- Guide to Law Online British Virgin Islands, Law Library of Congress (https://guides.loc.gov/law-british-virgin-islands, accessed May 30, 2022).
- Hendry, I. D., and Dickson, Susan. *British Overseas Territories Law*. Oxford: Hart, 2018.
- Maurer, Bill. *Recharting the Caribbean: Land, Law, and Citizenship in the British Virgin Islands*. Ann Arbor: University of Michigan Press, 2000.
- Trotman, Donald A. B. *Revised Laws of the Virgin Islands*. Portsmouth: Grosvenor Press, 1991.

Cayman Islands

The Cayman Islands are a British Overseas Territory. In June 1863, it became a dependent of the Crown Colony of Jamaica. Its administration and governance continued until Jamaica gained its independence in 1962. The territory includes the following three islands: Grand Cayman, Cayman Brac, and Little Cayman. There is no specific agency or ministry responsible for local government. However, an authoritative place to start is the official Cayman Islands Government page (https://www.gov.ky/index.html, accessed May 30, 2022). The following resources are also helpful:

- *Cayman Islands Consolidated Index of Statutes and Subsidiary Legislation to 1st January 2005.* Law Revision Commissioner, Cayman Islands Government.
- *Cayman Islands Law Reports.* Oxford Law Reports International, 2020.
- *Cayman Islands Laws and Regulations Current to December 1988.* Government of the Cayman Islands, 1989.
- Davies, Elizabeth W. *The Legal System of the Cayman Islands.* Oxford: Law Reports International, 1989.
- Guide to Law Online Cayman Islands, Law Library of Congress (https://guides.loc.gov/law-cayman-islands/legal-guides, accessed May 30, 2022).
- Hendry, I. D., and Dickson, Susan. *British Overseas Territories Law.* Oxford: Hart, 2018.
- *Regulations, Rules and Orders of the Cayman Islands, 1964–1967.* National Government Publication. (This resource is not current, but it is useful for legislative history research.)

Commonwealth of Dominica

The Commonwealth of Dominica became a republic upon its independence from Britain in 1978. The country is divided into ten parishes. Dominica.gov (https://dominica.gov.dm/, accessed May 30, 2022) is the gateway to its laws. The following resources are also helpful:

- *Commonwealth of Dominica Consolidated Index of Statutes and Subsidiary Legislation to 1st January 2015*. Cave Hill: Faculty of Law, University of the West Indies.
- Guide to Law Online Dominica, Law Library of Congress (https://guides.loc.gov/law-dominica, accessed May 30, 2022).
- Harris, Francis Otho Coleridge. *Laws of Dominica*. Roseau: Government of the Commonwealth of Dominica, 1991.
- *Proposals for New Policies and Legislation Adjustments*. Roseau: Dominica Inland Revenue Department, 1995.

Grenada

Grenada is divided into seven parishes, and this includes the islands of Carriacou and Petite Martinique. There is no local government in Grenada. However, its constitution states that there should be a local government council on Carriacou and Petite Martinique. The Carriacou and Petite Martinique Council Act 1995 is expected to provide for this constitutional objective. There is also a Ministry of Carriacou and Petite Martinique Affairs. In 2015, there was a referendum on local governance, but it did not receive public support.

The following are additional print and online sources for researching the laws of Grenada:

- Alexa, Francis. *The Continuous Revised Edition of the Laws of Grenada*. St. George's: Government of Grenada, 1994.

- *Grenada Consolidated Index of Statutes and Subsidiary Legislation to 1st January 2014*. Cave Hill: Faculty of Law, University of the West Indies.
- Guide to Law Online Grenada, Law Library of Congress (https://guides.loc.gov/law-grenada, accessed May 30, 2022).
- *Laws of Grenada*. St. George's: Government Printing Office, 2000.
- *The Revised Laws of Grenada: The Statutes in Force on the 31st of December 1990*. St. George's: Government of Grenada.

Guyana

Governance in Guyana is at the national, regional, and local levels, with local government outlined in Chapter VII, Section 71(1) of the constitution. The two main legislations related to local governance are the Municipal and District Councils Act of 1988 and the Local Government Act of 1988. The Ministry of Communities oversees an extensive local government structure that consists of ten regional development councils, six municipalities, and sixty-five neighborhood democratic councils. In addition, there are approximately seventy-five Amerindian village councils.

The Government of Guyana has a very comprehensive database on subsidiary legislation (https://parliament.gov.gy/publications/subsidiary-legislation/, accessed May 30, 2022).

The following documents are accessible:

- Bulkan, Arif. *The Survival of Indigenous Rights in Guyana*. University of Guyana, 2018.
- Guide to Law Online Guyana, Law Library of Congress (https://guides.loc.gov/law-guyana, accessed May 30, 2022).

- *Guyana Consolidated Index of Statutes and Subsidiary Legislation to 1st January 2011*. Faculty of Law, University of the West Indies, 2011
- The Laws of Guyana 2000. Ministry of Legal Affairs, Government of Guyana, 2002. (This is in loose-leaf format, with updates.)
- Local Government, Ministry of Local Government and Regional Development (https://mlgrd.gov.gy/local-government/, accessed May 30, 2022).
- Proclamations, Regulations, Rules, Orders, By-Laws, and Notices. There is also a section on Motions (https://parliament.gov.gy/publications/motions/, accessed May 30, 2022).

Jamaica

In Jamaica the Ministry of Local Government and Rural Development (https://www.localgovjamaica.gov.jm/, accessed May 30, 2022) is a source for researching municipal laws. There are links to Acts of Parliament (https://www.localgovjamaica.gov.jm/resources/?category=8, accessed May 30, 2022) and updates on local government reform. Jamaica comprises fourteen parishes, and there has been a recent proposal by the Ministry of Local Government and Rural Development to make Portmore, the largest dormitory community in the English-speaking Caribbean, Jamaica's fifteenth parish. Each parish has a municipal corporation that provides governance. Municipal laws can be located on municipality websites. Currency of the information will vary from parish to parish.

Some important statutes related to local governance in Jamaica are:

- Local Governance Act, 2016
- Local Government (Financing and Financial Management) Act, 2016

- Local Government (Unified Service and Employment) Act, 2016
- The Town and Country Planning Act of 1958 (amended January 1, 1999)

The following are further resources to facilitate the research of Jamaican municipal laws:

- Guide to Law Online Jamaica, Law Library of Congress (https://guides.loc.gov/law-jamaica, accessed May 30, 2022).
- The Local Government System in Jamaica Commonwealth Local Government Forum (http://www.clgf.org.uk/default/assets/File/Country_profiles/Jamaica.pdf, accessed February 25, 2021).
- Robinson, Leacroft. *The Laws of Jamaica: Subsidiary Legislation*. Montrose Printery, 1990.

Montserrat

Montserrat is an Overseas Territory of the United Kingdom. Between 1958 and 1962, it was a part of the Federation of the West Indies. The premier is the head of government. There are three parishes—St. Peter, St. Georges, and St. Anthony—but there is no local government structure in place at this time. The following sources are helpful for researching the law of Montserrat:

- Attorney General's Chambers, Acts (http://agc.gov.ms/?page_id=352, accessed May 30, 2022).
- Guide to Law Online Montserrat, Law Library of Congress (https://guides.loc.gov/law-montserrat, accessed May 30, 2022).
- *Montserrat Consolidated Index of Statutes and Subsidiary Legislation to 1st January 2003*. Faculty of Law, Cave Hill, University of the West Indies, 2008.

St. Kitts and Nevis

The twin-island state of St. Kitts and Nevis does not have a designated ministry for local government. Chapter X of its constitution addresses the island of Nevis, including Nevis island administration. The official government website (https://www.gov.kn/, accessed May 30, 2022) does have a link to its documents center, which can facilitate research. The following acts and ordinances are available online through the Law Commission (http://www.lawcommission.gov.kn/, accessed May 30, 2022), an arm of the Ministry of Justice and Legal Affairs (https://www.legal.gov.kn/, accessed May 30, 2022):

- Annual Laws of St. Kitts and Nevis
    - The Revised Acts of St. Kitts and Nevis at 31st December, 2017 (Supplement)
    - The Revised Acts of St. Kitts and Nevis at 31st December, 2009
- Ordinances of Nevis
    - Revised Ordinances of Nevis as at 31st December, 2017 (Supplement)
    - Revised Ordinances of Nevis as at 31st December, 2009
- Guide to Law Online, St. Kitts and Nevis, Law Library of Congress (https://www.loc.gov/item/guide-to-law-online/saint-kitts-and-nevis/, accessed May 30, 2022)

St. Lucia

The island of St. Lucia is divided into eleven quarters (commonly known as parishes in other islands). The quarters are: Anse la Raye, Castries, Choiseul, Dauphin, Dennery, Gros Islet, Laborie, Micoud, Praslin, Soufriere, and Vieux Fort. St. Lucia's ministry for local governance is the Ministry of Equity, Social Justice, Local Government, and Empowerment. The government's Publications (http://www.govt.lc/publications/, accessed May 30, 2022) section is searchable by resource type (legislation, forms, publications), and by ministry, topic, or audience. For locating legislation by ministry or department, consult the Attorney General's Chambers page (https://attorneygeneralchambers.com/p/legislation-by-ministry-or-department, accessed May 30, 2022). Additional resources include:

- Guide to Law Online St. Lucia, Law Library of Congress (https://www.loc.gov/item/guide-to-law-online/saint-lucia/, accessed May 30, 2022).
- *Laws of St. Lucia Complete Set*. Butterworths, 2014.
- *Laws of Saint Lucia: Comprising All of the Acts and Subsidiary Legislation in Force on 31 December 2001*. Eyre and Spottiswoode, 2001.
- *Saint Lucia. Consolidated Index of Statutes and Subsidiary Legislation to 1st January 2017*. Faculty of Law, University of the West Indies, Cave Hill, 2017.

St. Vincent and the Grenadines

St. Vincent and the Grenadines is divided into six parishes: Charlotte, Grenadines, St. Andrew, St. David, St. George, and St. Patrick. There is no constitutional provision for local-level government. Rather, clerks are appointed to head each parish. The Local Authorities (Termination of Dissolution) Act of 1981 guides local administration.

From the website of the Ministry of Legal Affairs (https://legal.gov.vc/legal/, accessed May 30, 2022), acts, bills, and policies are accessible. There is also a Publications page (https://finance.gov.vc/finance/index.php/publications-and-reports, accessed May 30, 2022) containing ministerial statements, fiscal summaries, reports, and contract awards. Other resources include:

- Guide to Law Online St. Vincent and the Grenadines, Law Library of Congress (https://www.loc.gov/item/guide-to-law-online/saint-vincent-and-the-grenadines/, accessed May 30, 2022).
- *The Laws of St. Vincent and the Grenadines: In Force on the 1st January, 1991*. Government of St. Vincent and the Grenadines, 1992.
- *Saint Vincent and the Grenadines Consolidated Index of Statutes and Subsidiary Legislation to 1st January 1991 Bridgetown, Barbados: Faculty of Law Library.*

Trinidad and Tobago

The territory of Trinidad and Tobago is a parliamentary republic with two levels of government. Trinidad is divided into fourteen municipalities/regional corporations, while Tobago has a single House of Assembly. The Ministry of Rural Development and Local Government is responsible for local governance. There is no constitutional provision for local government in Trinidad and Tobago. However, the Tobago House of Assembly is set out in Chapter 11A of the constitution.

The Municipal Corporations Act of 1990 and the Tobago House of Assembly Act of 1996 are key legislations relating to local government. The Transitioning of Local Government Policy was drafted in 2016 and proposes some legislative changes relating to the operations of the councils, further decentralization, and expansion, among other issues. Additional resources include:

- Guide to Law Online Trinidad and Tobago, Law Library of Congress (https://www.loc.gov/item/guide-to-law-online/trinidad-and-tobago/, accessed May 30, 2022)
- Local Government of Trinidad and Tobago (https://www.commonwealthgovernance.org/countries/americas/trinidad_and_tobago/local-government/, accessed May 30, 2022)

- *Republic of Trinidad and Tobago Consolidated Index of Public Acts and Subsidiary Legislation to 1st January 1996.* Faculty of Law, University of the West Indies, Cave Hill, 1996

Turks and Caicos Islands

Turks and Caicos Islands is a British Overseas Territory. Part X, 130 of The Turks and Caicos Islands Constitution Order 2011 (https://www.legislation.gov.uk/uksi/2011/1681/made, accessed May 30, 2022) provides for "the establishment and functions of local councils to contribute to effective local government in the islands." Local governance falls under the Office of the Premier, Local Government, and Community Affairs. An appointed governor is the head of state. There are five administrative districts: Providenciales, North Caicos, Middle Caicos, and South Caicos that are located in the Caicos Islands, and Salt Cay is located in the Turks Islands. Each administrative district is managed by a district commissioner. However, Providenciales is managed by the permanent secretary in the Office of the Premier. The island of Grand Turk is administered directly by the Turks and Caicos government. For a more detailed structure of the government, see the official government website (https://www.gov.tc/government, accessed May 30, 2022).

In 2019, the Local Government Review and Modernisation Committee began public consultations with the aim of local government reform.

Additional resources on the laws of the Turks and Caicos Islands are below:

- Adsett, Neil James. *Laws of the Turks and Caicos Islands: Comprising All of the Ordinances, Subsidiary Legislation and Certain Other Laws in Force on 15 May 1998.* Government of the Turks and Caicos Islands, 1998.
- Guide to Law Online Turks and Caicos Islands, Law Library of Congress (https://www.loc.gov/item/guide-to-law-online/turks-and-caicos/, accessed May 30, 2022).

- Hendry, I. D., and Dickson, Susan. *British Overseas Territories Law*. Oxford: Hart, 2018.
- *The Laws of the Turks and Caicos Islands*. Attorney General's Chambers, 1998 onwards. (This is a continually updated loose-leaf publication.)
- *Turks and Caicos Islands: Consolidated Index and Statutes of Subsidiary Legislation to 1st January 2001*. Faculty of Law, University of the West Indies, Cave Hill, Barbados.

References

Commonwealth Secretariat. *Local Democracy and Good Governance in the Caribbean: Report of the Regional Symposium Held in Montego Bay, Jamaica*. April 2004.

Cramer, Winston, and Persaud, Patricia. *Decentralization and Local Government in the Caribbean*. Washington, DC: National Democratic Institute for International Affairs, 2004.

Government at a Glance: Latin America and the Caribbean 2020. Paris: OECD Publishing. https://doi.org/10.1787/13130fbb-en (accessed May 30, 2022).

Kerley, Richard, Liddle, Joyce, and Dunning, Pam, Eds. *The Routledge Handbook of International Local Government*. Abingdon: Routledge, 2019.

Minto-Coy, Indianna D., and Berman, Evan M. *Public Administration and Policy in the Caribbean*. Boca Raton: CRC Press, 2016.

Ragoonath, B. "Local Governance in the Caribbean." In *Global Encyclopedia of Public Administration, Public Policy, and Governance*, edited by A. Farazmand. Cham: Springer, 2019.

Sansom, Graham, and McKinlay, Peter. *New Century Local Government: Commonwealth Perspectives*. London: Commonwealth Secretariat, 2013.

Chapter 6

Legislative History

The aim of legislative history research is to ascertain the legislative intent at the time that the legislation was being drafted and to be able to trace changes to legislation over time through a review of the documentary trail involved in the legislative process. Some of the main documents involved would include committee reports, bills, debates, testimonies, and other secondary sources to determine any social, political, or economic contexts relating to the legislation. This section will highlight some possible sources that can facilitate Caribbean legislative history. As well, general legislative history tools for research beyond the Caribbean will be outlined.

It is helpful to start with the official website of the state or territory. This is where you are likely to find links to resource or document centers, committees, bills, reports, and press releases. Focus on department pages of the cabinet secretary, justice department, attorney general, or their equivalent in each territory. One helpful resource is Digital Library of the Caribbean (https://dloc.com/collections/dloh, accessed May 30, 2022). It contains legal materials from 1766 to 2015 in multiple languages from sources such as official gazettes and newspapers.

Sources for West Indies Federation and Other Pre- and Postindependence Legal Documents

Though short lived, the interlude of West Indian federalism in the 1950s generated a wealth of documents that can facilitate research of preindependence referenda, Caribbean constitutionalism, federalism, and other legal history topics. Included here are some of those main sources, most notably Her Majesty's Stationery Office, which include acts, law reports, committee reports, and conference proceedings. Please see the chapter on treaty research for an in-depth discussion of relevant pre- and postindependence Caribbean treaties.

Acts

British Caribbean Federation Act, 1956. Her Majesty's Stationery Office, 1956.

Bills

British Caribbean Federation Bill. Her Majesty's Stationery Office, 1956.

Gazette

The West Indies Gazette. Legal Supplement: Appendix: Commencement of Federation. The West Indies Gazette, 1958.

Law Reports

The West Indian Law Reports. Lexis-Nexis, 2020. (Previously published by Butterworths, coverage is from 1959 to present. There are ample materials on West Indies federation and preindependence law reports that are useful for legislative history research.)

Reports

Report of the Conference on Movement of Persons within a British Caribbean Federation Held in Port of Spain, Trinidad from Monday 14th March to Thursday 17th March 1955. Her Majesty's Stationery Office, 1955.

Report by the Conference on West Indian Federation Held in London in April 1953. London Her Majesty's Stationery Office, 1953.

Report of the East Caribbean Federation Conference 1962. Her Majesty's Stationery Office, 1963.

The Plan for a British Caribbean Federation. Report of the Judicial Commissioner. Colonial Office. British Caribbean Federation Judicial Commission. Her Majesty's Stationery Office, 1956.

General Legislative History Research Sources

Listed below are some general legislative history research sources that are not Caribbean specific, but which can provide further guidance on enhancing legislative research skills.

- Federal Legislative History: Initial Steps, Law Library of Congress (https://www.loc.gov/law/help/leghist.php, accessed May 30, 2022).
- Georgetown Law Library Legislative Research Guide (https://guides.ll.georgetown.edu/legislative_history, accessed May 30, 2022).
- Law Librarian Society of Washington, DC, Legislative Sourcebook (https://www.llsdc.org/sourcebook, accessed May 30, 2022).
- McKinney, Richard J., and Sweet, Ellen. *Federal Legislative History Research: A Practitioner's Guide to Compiling the Documents and Sifting for Legislative Intent*. Law Librarians' Society of Washington, DC, 2006.

- Taylor, Julia. *Legislative History Research: A Basic Guide.* Washington, DC: Congressional Research Service, 2011.

References

Berry, David S. *Caribbean Integration Law.* Oxford: Oxford University Press, 2014.

Caribbean Free Trade Association. *Agreement and Related Documents.* Caribbean Free Trade Association, 1970.

Collins, Justine K. *Tracing British West Indian Slavery Laws: A Comparative Analysis of Legal Transplants.* Abingdon: Routledge, 2021.

Geiser, Hans Jorg, Alleyne, Pamela, and Gajraj, Caroll. *Legal Problems of Caribbean Integration: A Study on the Legal Aspects of CARICOM.* Institute of International Relations, Sijthoff, 1976.

Hornbeck, J. F. *CARICOM: Challenges and Opportunities for Caribbean Economic Integration.* Washington, DC: Congressional Research Service, Library of Congress, 2008.

Madden, Frederick, and Darwin, John. *End of Empire: Dependencies since 1948: The West Indies, British Honduras, Hong Kong, Fiji, Cyprus, Gibraltar, and the Falklands: Select Documents on the Constitutional History of the British Empire and Commonwealth.* Westport: ABC-CLIO, 2000. (This is also available as an e-book.)

Mawby, Spencer. *Ordering Independence: The End of Empire in the Anglophone Caribbean: 1947–1969.* Palgrave MacMillan, 2014.

Meeks, Brian, Quinn, Kate, and Barrow-Giles, Cynthia. *Beyond Westminster in the Caribbean.* Kingston: Ian Randle Publishers, 2018.

Organisation of Eastern Caribbean States. *Forms of Political Union—A Discussion Paper on a Union to Suit Our Needs: Federation? Confederation? Unitary State? Another Form?* Castries: OECS Secretariat, 1988.

Wallace, Elisabeth M. *The British Caribbean: From the Decline of Colonialism to the End of Federation*. Toronto: University of Toronto Press, 2019.

Chapter 7

Researching Case Law

Law reporting in the Caribbean dates back to the early 1900s while case law from the colonial period is published in English reports. Case law publishing is still predominantly in print. Some jurisdictions make their law reports available through their government printers while others are from commercial services. Case law has also been published in gazettes.

This chapter lists selected sources of case law research for the English-speaking Caribbean countries. The University of the West Indies Law Library has a very extensive collection of law reports and sources for researching case law for the English-speaking countries.

The following are selected law reports and sources for researching case law:

- *Law Reports of the Bahamas* (Butterworths) provides coverage from 1965 to 1980, and 1987 to 1990. It covers cases from the Court of Appeal, Supreme Court, and magistrate courts.
- *Barbados Law Reports* (Gaunt) covers 1948 to present. It covers Superior Courts of Barbados and the West Indian Court of Appeal on appeal from Barbados.

- *Barbados Reports 1897–1903*, Volumes 1 (1694–1893) and 2 (1894–1903) (T. E. King and Co.) cover selected cases from local courts in Barbados and the Windward Islands Court of Appeal.
- Decisions of the Supreme Court of Barbados.
- *Bermuda Law Reports* Volume 1, 1904–1924, and Volume 2, 1925–1926.
- Bermuda Laws Online (http://www.bermudalaws.bm/SitePages/Home.aspx, accessed May 26, 2022) is a government website that provides access to annual laws and consolidated laws from 1993 to date.
- *Caribbean Commercial Law Reports* Volumes 1 and 2 cover the period 1988–1989. Cases in this volume cover admiralty, arbitration, company, contracts, tax, industrial, insurance, and revenue. Its scope includes the superior courts in Belize, the Bahamas, Barbados, Cayman Islands, Grenada, Jamaica, Trinidad and Tobago, Turks and Caicos Islands, and countries under the Eastern Caribbean Court of Appeal.
- The Caribbean Court of Justice provides access to judgments with respect to its Original Jurisdiction (https://www.ccj.org/judgments-proceedings/original-jurisdiction-judgments/, accessed May 26, 2022) as well as Appellate Jurisdiction Judgments (https://www.ccj.org/judgments-proceedings/appellate-jurisdiction-judgments/, accessed May 26, 2022).
- *Cayman Islands Law Reports 1952 to Present*. The print volumes are published by Law Reports International. Unreported cases and selected judgments are available by subscription from the website of the Cayman Islands Judicial Administration Department (https://www.judicial.ky/judgments, accessed May 26, 2022).

- Eastern Caribbean Supreme Court (https://www.eccourts.org/category/judgments/, accessed May 26, 2022) provides cases heard before the Court of Appeal and the High Court of Justice of the Eastern Caribbean Supreme Court.
- *Jamaica Law Reports* (Caribbean Law Publishing Company) prints reports of cases heard before Jamaican courts for 1934–1994, 1977–1994, and 1995 to present.
- *Trinidad & Tobago Law Reports* (Government Printing Office) covers cases for the period 1913–1979 and published by the Government Printing Office. Another version published by the Caribbean Law Publishing Company covers cases for the period of 1990–1995.
- Judiciary of Trinidad and Tobago (https://www.ttlawcourts.org/#, accessed May 26, 2022) covers cases from the Supreme Court, Court of Appeal, High Court, Family Court, and Magistrate Courts. The Law Library of the Judiciary provides access to indexes and abstracts of cases for the Supreme Court of Trinidad and Tobago from 1990.
- *Organisation of Eastern Caribbean States (OECS) Law Reports/Judgments* is a three-volume set. Publishing commenced in 1991 on judgments of the superior courts of the OECS. See the Eastern Caribbean Supreme Court (https://www.eccourts.org/judgments, accessed May 26, 2022).
- *Law Reports of the Commonwealth* (Butterworths) covers judgments of selected jurisdictions of the English-speaking Caribbean.
- *West Indian Law Reports* (Butterworths) coverage is from 1958 for cases from the Bahamas and Barbados.
- Judicial Committee of the Privy Council (https://www.jcpc.uk/cases/index.html, accessed May 26, 2022).

- Historical Cases: Selected historical cases for the Bahamas, Barbados, and Jamaica are available on LLMC Digital by subscription.

Case law for United Kingdom Overseas Territories, Crown Dependencies, and some independent Caribbean states can be found on the website of the Judicial Committee of the Privy Council since it is the final court of final appeal for these jurisdictions .

Sources for Updating Cases

This section will discuss the importance of updating cases and will outline some of the tools that are available for ensuring that current case law is cited. Within the Caribbean, there are limited options in terms of print and electronic resources for updating cases. However, a number of sources for checking the status of a case, such as digests, and indexes are available in the United Kingdom. It is important to also remember that for Jamaica and several other Caribbean states, the Judicial Committee of the Privy Council is still the body of last resort, instead of the Caribbean Court of Justice, so these decisions will also be useful to determine a case's status.

Once a case has been decided, it can be:

(a) Reversed on appeal,
(b) Criticized, and/or
(c) Overruled by subsequent cases.

To determine whether a particular case is still relevant, or good law, it is important to update the case. The term "noting up" is generally used for the updating process. Online legal databases such as Westlaw and Lexis also have online citators such as KeyCite and Shepard to help users determine the status of cases and statutes.

Below are some of the sources that will facilitate updating of cases.

Caribbean Updating Sources

Caribbean Court of Justice (https://ccj.org/judgments-proceedings/, accessed May 30, 2022). The Caribbean Court of Justice is a free source for finding appellate jurisdiction and original jurisdiction judgments.

Caribbean Law Project on CommonLii (http://www.commonlii.org/resources/55912/, accessed May 30, 2022).

Eastern Caribbean Supreme Court Digests of Decisions (https://www.eccourts.org/category/digests-of-decisions/, accessed May 30, 2022). The Digests of Decisions is searchable by year and country. Coverage of cases is from 2006 to 2018.

United Kingdom Updating Sources

Bailii.org (British and Irish Legal Information Institute) (https://www.bailii.org/, accessed May 30, 2022). Although coverage is mainly focused on British and Irish materials, Bailii is still a helpful resource for finding current information on cases and legislation.

Judicial Committee of the Privy Council (https://www.jcpc.uk/, accessed May 30, 2022). Since Jamaica and a few other Caribbean states still rely on the Judicial Committee of the Privy Council as the court of last resort, this is a helpful source to check the status of cases. Coverage for decided cases is from 2009 to 2020. Users can also review current cases before the Privy Council. Current cases can be searched by case ID, case name, or jurisdiction.

Other Sources

vLex Caribbean Collection (https://vlex.com/coverage/carilaw-caribbean-law, accessed May 30, 2022, and August 19, 2023). This collection was previously under the platform JustisOne. In 2017 it migrated to vLex Justis Carilaw Collection, with approximately 50,000 cases from 18 jurisdictions. Content types include cases, administrative decisions, digests, and dockets. It is subscription based.

LexisNexis Butterworths and Westlaw. Although limited, both LexisNexis Butterworths and Westlaw have resources for updating Caribbean cases. Westlaw contains judgments from both the High Court and Court of Appeal of the Eastern Caribbean Supreme Court.

Chapter 8

Caribbean Courts, Court Rules, and General Court Documents

This chapter will discuss court structure and outline sources for locating court rules and general court documents. It will also review the courts of last resort for these territories, such as the Caribbean Court of Justice (CCJ) and the Judicial Committee of the Privy Council (JCPC). For a more logical structure, the court systems of Barbados, Belize, the Bahamas, the Cayman Islands, Guyana, Jamaica, Trinidad and Tobago, and the Turks and Caicos Islands will be looked at individually, while the court structures in the six independent states (Antigua and Barbuda, Commonwealth of Dominica, Grenada, St. Kitts and Nevis, St. Vincent and the Grenadines, St. Lucia) and the three British Overseas Territories (Anguilla, British Virgin Islands, and Montserrat) that fall under the jurisdiction of the Eastern Caribbean Supreme Court will be reviewed as a group.

While most of these states have similar court structures (mainly a three-tier structure with magistrates' courts at the base) and court rules, there are unique features, depending on history, geography, and governance structure. Guyana, for example, has a mixed system, and there are special conditions related to British Overseas

Territories. With respect to judicial appointments, again there are variations, but usually, appointments are made by governors or governors general, in keeping with guidelines of Judicial Service Commissions. Therefore, when researching court rules or general court documents, it is best to consult the specific court's website or the website of the ministerial authority for justice in the territory that you are researching. An attempt has been made in this chapter to provide links to as many of these websites as possible.

The Bahamas

The Bahamas has fifteen Magistrate's Courts in New Providence. They include a Drug Court, Firearms Court, Coroner's Court, Night Civil Court, and two Night Traffic Courts. In Gran Bahama, there are four Magistrate's Courts, while Abaco has one such court. The Supreme Court has twelve justices, including the chief justice. The Court of Appeal is the highest court, and it sits full-time throughout the year. Its jurisdiction includes criminal, civil, and constitutional issues. The JCPC is the court of last resort for the Bahamas.

Barbados

Barbados has a three-tier structure with Magistrates' Courts, and the Supreme Court of Judicature comprises the High Court and Court of Appeal. The Caribbean Court of Justice is Barbados's court of last resort. Magistrates' Courts cover Districts A through F across the island, and they can hear cases relating to civil, family, and criminal matters, as well as contract and tort cases where claims do not exceed $10,000.

Belize

Belize has a three-tier court structure: Magistrate's Courts (of which there are nine) and Family Court, Court of Appeal, and the Supreme Court of Judicature, which is governed by the Supreme Court of Judicature Act. Previously, the JCPC was the court of last resort for Belize. However, the 2009 constitutional amendment allowed for Belize's accession to the appellate jurisdiction of the CCJ effective June 1, 2010. For more information on Belize's judicial system, see https://www.belizejudiciary.org/ (accessed May 30, 2022).

Cayman Islands

The Cayman Islands court structure includes the Summary Court, Grand Court, Court of Appeal, and the JCPC. The Summary Court has jurisdiction over all civil and criminal matters. A Drug Treatment Court was established within the Summary Court in October 2007. The Grand Court was originally created as a court of special limited jurisdiction in 1877. The Grand Court Law of 1975 established the modern court, and it hears both criminal and civil appeals from the Summary Court.

Appeals from the Grand Court go to the Court of Appeal. The Court of Appeal, like the Grand Court, is a Superior Court of Record. It was established in 1984. Prior to 1984, the Court of Appeal of Jamaica heard appeals from the Cayman Islands.

The JCPC is the final appellate court for the Cayman Islands, and appeals from the Court of Appeal are heard there.

Guyana

Guyana's history as a former Dutch colony reflects its mixed legal system of civil and common law. It has nine magisterial districts, and the Magistrates' Act governs its Magistrate Courts. These courts are the largest in number and deal with civil claims of small value and minor offences. Magistrates' jurisdictions extend to presiding over specialized courts such as Family Court, Commercial Court, Coroner's Court, Juvenile Court, Traffic Court, Tax Court, and Drug Court.

Guyana's Supreme Court has two divisions—the Court of Appeal and the High Court of the Supreme Court of Judicature. The High Court hears claims exceeding $50,000 and deals with family law, probate, as well as mortgages and titles through a Land Court.

In 2005, Guyana replaced the JCPC with the CCJ as its final court of appeal.

Jamaica

In Jamaica, Resident Magistrates' courts are at the parish level, and these courts deal with civil and criminal offences that are less serious. Jamaica also has special courts, namely, Traffic Court, Family Court, Revenue Court, Petty Sessions Courts, and Gun Court. Petty Sessions Courts are presided over by justices of the peace and deal with minor offences. Jamaica is perhaps the only Caribbean state with a Gun Court. Parliament established the Gun Court in 1974 to address increasing gun violence. There are two such courts—one in Kingston, and the other in Montego Bay—and they deal with criminal cases involving firearms.

Trinidad and Tobago

Trinidad and Tobago's court structure comprises the Supreme Court of Judicature (High Court and Court of Appeal) and the Magistracy. The High Court has three divisions, namely Matrimonial, Criminal, and Civil. The Magistracy is divided into thirteen districts. The Court of Appeal hears appeals from the Magistracy and the High Court. The JCPC is the court of last resort for Trinidad and Tobago.

Turks and Caicos Islands

The Turks and Caicos Islands' court structure consists of Magistrates' Courts on Providenciales and Grand Turk, as well as the Supreme Court, which is similar to the High Court in England, and the Court of Appeals. The Supreme Court hears appeals from the Magistrates' Courts. Like most other Caribbean states, the JCPC is the court of last resort. The governor appoints judges to the Supreme Court and the Court of Appeals.

The Eastern Caribbean Supreme Court

The Eastern Caribbean Supreme Court, formerly referred to as the West Indies Associated States Supreme Court, has its genesis in the West Indies Act of 1967. The aim of the act was to "establish common courts for the group of Associated States," (Eastern Caribbean Supreme Court website, accessed June 21, 2021). This association of states would later become more widely known as the Organisation of Eastern Caribbean States (OECS). The West Indies Associated States Supreme Court Order later allowed for the merging of the High Court and the Court of Appeal into the Supreme Court.

The court's main functions are the following:

(1) To interpret and apply the laws of the OECS;

(2) To decide civil and criminal cases; and

(3) To hear appeals.

Courts of Last Resort

Judicial Committee of the Privy Council

The JCPC is the court of final appeal for United Kingdom Overseas Territories, Crown Dependencies, and Commonwealth countries that have retained the appeal to the JCPC. Its origins date back to 1833 at the zenith of the British Empire, during which it was the highest court of civil and criminal appeal. The judges of the JCPC are normally justices of the United Kingdom Supreme Court. Five judges usually sit to hear appeals from the Commonwealth.

Currently, the JCPC, based in England, serves as the court of last resort for most Caribbean states.

Caribbean Court of Justice

Throughout this work, the history, role, and functions of the CCJ have been discussed. At the time of writing, it is currently the final court of appeal for Barbados, Belize, and Guyana. Established in 2001 and headquartered in Trinidad and Tobago, it is a hybrid court—a court of last resort, and vested with original jurisdiction regarding interpretation and application of the Revised Treaty of Chaguaramas. There is a substantial body of work on the CCJ, and extensive analysis on the reasons for hesitancy among so many Caribbean states on its acceptance as a court of last resort. In this chapter and in others, attempts have been made to include several resources relating to the court.

Court Rules and Practice Directions

Listed below are links to various court websites and their Rules of Court and Practice Directions.

- Barbados Judicial System Rules of Court (https://www.barbadoslawcourts.gov.bb/rules-of-court/, accessed May 30, 2022)
- Belize Judiciary Rules of Court (https://www.belizejudiciary.org/rules-of-the-court-2/, accessed May 30, 2022)
- Caribbean Court of Justice Rules of Court (https://www.ccj.org/court-instruments/rules-of-the-court/, accessed May 30, 2022)

- Caribbean Court of Justice Original Jurisdiction Rules (https://www.ccj.org/court-instruments/rules-of-the-court/the-original-jurisdiction-rules/, accessed May 30, 2022)
- Caribbean Court of Justice Appellate Jurisdiction Rules (https://www.ccj.org/court-instruments/rules-of-the-court/the-appellate-jurisdiction-rules/, accessed May 30, 2022)
- Caribbean Court of Justice Practice Directions (https://www.ccj.org/court-instruments/rules-of-the-court/practice-directions/, accessed May 30, 2022)
- Cayman Islands Court Rules (https://www.judicial.ky/courts/court-rules-all, accessed May 30, 2022)
- Eastern Caribbean Supreme Court (https://www.eccourts.org/, accessed May 30, 2022). From the Civil Procedure & Rules tab, there are links to many of the court rules. There is also an E-Litigation Filing and Service Procedure Rules (https://www.eccourts.org/electronic-litigation-filing-and-service-procedure-rules/, accessed May 30, 2022) link providing guidance on electronic filing for the individual territories.
- The Judicial Committee of the Privy Council (https://www.jcpc.uk/index.html, accessed May 30, 2022). Its Practice Directions (https://www.jcpc.uk/procedures/practice-directions.html, accessed May 30, 2022) are available, and the Rules of the Committee (https://www.jcpc.uk/procedures/rules-of-the-committee.html, accessed May 30, 2022) are current to 2009.
- Supreme Court of Jamaica Rules of Court (https://supreme-court.gov.jm/content/rules-court, accessed May 30, 2022)

- Court of Appeals Jamaica. Practice Directions and Practice Notes (https://www.courtofappeal.gov.jm/content/practice-directions-and-practice-notes, accessed May 30, 2022)
- Trinidad and Tobago Supreme Court Rules (http://www.ttlawcourts.org/index.php/rules-a-practice-directions/supreme-court, accessed May 30, 2022)
- Trinidad and Tobago Family Court Rules (http://www.ttlawcourts.org/index.php/rules-a-practice-directions/family-court, accessed May 30, 2022)

References

Adams, Errol A. *Guyana Law and Legal Research.* 2020. New York: Globalex, New York University, 2020. https://www.nyulawglobal.org/globalex/Guyana.html (accessed June 2021).

Alexis, Francis. *Eastern Caribbean Supreme Court: Model Regional Court.* Eastern Caribbean Supreme Court, 2007.

Cabatingan, Lee. *A Region among States: Law and Sovereignty in the Caribbean.* Chicago: The University of Chicago Press, 2023.

The Caribbean Civil Court Practice. Bahamas Supplement, 2012. LexisNexis, 2014.

Caribbean Community Secretariat. *The Caribbean Court of Justice: How the Court Works. Original Jurisdiction.* Georgetown: Caribbean Community Secretariat, 2005.

Caribbean Court of Justice. *The Caribbean Court of Justice (Original Jurisdiction) Rules.* Port of Spain: Caribbean Court of Justice, 2006.

Caserta, Salvatore. *International Courts in Latin America and the Caribbean: Foundations and Authority.* Oxford: Oxford University Press, 2021.

Civil Procedure Rules 2002. Jamaica Supreme Court. Kingston: Caribbean Law Publishing Company, 2006.

Deane, Catherine A. *Trinidad & Tobago Law and Legal Research.* 2020. New York: Globalex, New York University, 2020. https://www.nyulawglobal.org/globalex/Trinidad_Tobago1.html (accessed June 2021).

Di Mambro, David. *The Caribbean Civil Court Practice.* LexisNexis Butterworths 2011.

Eastern Caribbean Supreme Court Civil Procedure Rules 2000. Kingston: Caribbean Law Publishing, 2001. (This is in loose-leaf format, with periodic updates.)

Howell, P. A. *The Judicial Committee of the Privy Council 1833–1876: Its Origins, Structure and Development.* Cambridge: Cambridge University Press, 2009.

Jamaica Court of Appeals Rules. Kingston: Caribbean Law Publishing Company, 2002.

Swinfen, D. B. *Imperial Appeal: The Debate on the Appeal to the Privy Council, 1833–1986.* Manchester University Press, 1987.

Young, Harold A. *The Judicial Committee of the Privy Council and the Caribbean Court of Justice: Navigating Independence and Changing Political Environments.* Lanham: Lexington Books, 2021.

Chapter 9

Secondary Sources

In chapter 1, the importance of utilizing secondary sources in the research process was discussed, and examples of different types of secondary sources were provided in Table 1. In this chapter, we will focus on textbooks on various practice areas as well as other general titles related to Caribbean law. Over a two-year period (March 2020 to March 2022), the resources listed in WorldCat (worldcat.org) were reviewed and relevant titles are included below. Many of the resources listed in this chapter were written within the last five years, thereby providing current case law, legislation, and analysis, and also capturing emerging areas of law. Where resources that are a bit dated have been included, this is because there are currently no recent editions, or the work is seminal and can provide historical context for researchers.

Some important observations that emerged during the review on WorldCat include:

- The growing body of work on reparatory justice considering the ongoing strong push in the Caribbean for reparations from Britain for its former colonies;

- Many new titles on emerging topics such as climate change, cryptocurrencies, cybersecurity and data privacy, and drone law;
- The limited materials available on health law, particularly considering the COVID-19 pandemic's impact on the health and economic well-being of Caribbean states. It is hoped that more materials will be available shortly on health law, given issues that have emerged during the pandemic, such as the potential legal challenges to mandatory vaccination in the workplace, global health inequity, health informatics, and privacy;
- There were also no titles on election law in the Caribbean, even as several states have conducted electoral reforms, and the increasing push for local government. Hopefully, this area of law will receive attention soon; and
- Judicial review in the Caribbean had a fairly recent title, however, resources on independence of the judiciary and the judiciary and governance could benefit from more current titles.

Some annotations are provided for the resources. In some cases, titles are also available in e-book format.

General Sources

Antoine, Rose-Marie Belle. *The Rule of Law v. Ruling By Laws: Promoting Development in Caribbean Societies.* Port of Spain: Paria Publishing, 2018.

Johnson, Dexter Reno. *An Introduction to the Law and Legal System of the Bahamas.* The Bahamas: Terenshad Publishing, 2008.

Purdy, Jeannine M. *Common Law and Colonised Peoples: Studies in Trinidad and Western Australia.* Boca Raton: Routledge, 2020.

Practice Areas

Administrative Law

Bell, Joanna. *The Anatomy of Administrative Law*. Oxford: Hart Publishing, 2021.

Cane, Peter, Hofmann, Herwig C. H., Ip, Eric C., and Lindseth, Peter L. *The Oxford Handbook of Comparative Administrative Law*. Oxford: Oxford University Press, 2021.

Craig, Paul P. *Administrative Law*. London: Sweet and Maxwell, 2021.

Ventose, Eddy D. *Commonwealth Caribbean Administrative Law*. Abingdon: Routledge, 2020.

Wade, Henry William Rawson, and Forsyth, Christopher. *Administrative Law*. 11th ed. Oxford: Oxford University Press, 2014.

Alternative Dispute Resolution

Bevan, Alexander H. *Alternative Dispute Resolution: A Lawyer's Guide to Mediation and Other Forms of Dispute Resolution*. London: Sweet and Maxwell, 1992.

Blankley, Kristen M., and Weston, Maureen. *Understanding Alternative Dispute Resolution*. Durham: Carolina Academic Press, 2018.

Dragos, Dacian Cosmos, and Bogdana, Neamtu. *Alternative Dispute Resolution in Administrative Proceedings*. Heidelberg: Springer, 2014.

Fiadjoe, Albert. *Alternative Dispute Resolution: A Developing World Perspective*. London: Taylor and Francis, 2015.

Partridge, Mark V. B. *Alternative Dispute Resolution: An Essential Competency for Lawyers*. Oxford: Oxford University Press, 2009. (There is also a revised 2013 edition in e-book format, published by LexisNexis.)

Animal Law

Linzey, Andrew, and Linzey Clair, Eds. *Animal Ethics and Animal Law*. Lanham: Lexington Books, 2022.

Marceau, Justin. *Beyond Cages: Animal Law and Criminal Punishment*. Cambridge: Cambridge University Press, 2019.

Wagman, Bruce A., Waisman, Sonia, and Frasch, Pamela D. *Animal Law: Cases and Materials*. Durham: Carolina Academic Press, 2019.

Waisman, Sonia, Frasch, Pamela D., and Hessler, Katherine M. *Animal Law in a Nutshell*. 3rd ed. St. Paul: West Academic Publishing, 2021.

Zhang, Alex Xiaomeng, and Siler, Katherine. *Global Animal Law Research: Strategies and Resources*. Durham: Carolina Academic Press, 2022.

Aviation/Drone Law

Konert, Anna, and Kasprzyk, Piotr. *Drones—Future of Aviation Law?: Interference of Public Law in Private Law*. Berlin: Peter Lang, 2023.

Mignot-Mahdavi, Rebecca. *Drones and International Law: A Techno-Legal Machinery*. Cambridge: Cambridge University Press, 2023.

Schnitker, R. M., and Kaar, Dick van het. *Drone Law and Policy: Integration into the Legal Order of Civil Aviation*. The Hague: Eleven International Publishing, 2021.

Tarr, A. A., Tarr, Julie-Anne, Thompson, Maurice, and Ellis, Jeffrey. *Drone Law and Policy: Global Development, Risks, Regulation, and Insurance*. Abingdon: Routledge, 2021.

Banking and Financial Services Law

Antoine, Rose-Marie Belle. *Legal Issues in Offshore Financial Services*. Kingston: Caribbean Law Publishing Company, 2004.

Clarke, Rohan D. *Illicit Finance and the Law in the Commonwealth Caribbean: The Myth of Paradise*. Abingdon: Routledge, 2023.

Cranston, Ross, et al. *Principles of Banking Law*. 3rd ed. Oxford: Oxford University Press, 2018.

Gleeson, Simon. *Gleeson on the International Regulation of Banking*. 3rd ed. Oxford: Oxford University Press, 2018.

Haynes, Andrew. *The Law Related to International Banking*. 2nd ed. London: Bloomsbury Professional, 2018.

Olalla, Myriam Garcia, and Clifton, Judith. *Contemporary Issues in Banking: Regulation, Governance and Performance*. Cham: Palgrave Macmillan, 2019.

Paget, John R., and Odgers, John. *Paget's Law of Banking*. 15th ed. London: LexisNexis, 2018.

Business Law

Dobson, Alan P. *Charlesworth's Business Law*. 16th ed. London: Sweet and Maxwell, 1997.

Kelly, David, Hammer, Ruby, Denoncourt, Janice, and Hendy, John. *Business Law*. 4th ed. Abingdon: Routledge, 2021.

Ramlogan, Rajendra, and Persadie, Natalie Renee. *Commonwealth Caribbean Business Law*. Abingdon: Routledge, 2016.

Schaffer, Richard, Agusti, Filiberto, and Dhooge, Lucien J. *International Business Law and Its Environment*. Boston: Cengage Learning, 2022.

Slorach, J. Scott, and Ellis, Jason G. *Business Law*. 29th ed. Oxford: Oxford University Press, 2021.

Civil Procedure

DiMambro, David, Saunders, Adrian, and DiMambro, Louise. *The Caribbean Civil Court Practice*. London: LexisNexis, 2011.

Kodilinye, Gilbert, and Kodilinye, Vanessa. *Commonwealth Caribbean Civil Procedure*. 4th ed. Abingdon: Routledge, 2017.

Phillips, Fred. *Commonwealth Caribbean Civil Procedure*. (e-book). Milton: Taylor and Francis, 2013.

(Note: For more details on Caribbean courts, court rules, and general court documents, see chapter 8.)

Civil Rights

McIntosh, Simeon C. R. *Fundamental Rights and Democratic Governance*. Kingston: Ian Randle Publishers, 2005.

Mohamed, S. Y. *Fundamental Rights and Freedoms of the Commonwealth Caribbean*. Georgetown: New Guyana Company, 1993.

Newton, Velma. *Civil Rights with Special Reference to the Commonwealth Caribbean: A Select Bibliography*. Cave Hill: University of the West Indies, 1981.

Teelucksingh, Jerome. *Civil Rights in America and the Caribbean, 1950s–2010s*. Cham: Palgrave MacMillan, 2017.

Commercial Law

Kawaley, Ian, and Skiffington, Karen. *Offshore Commercial Law in Bermuda*. London: Wildy, Simmonds and Hill Publishing, 2018.

Lowe, Robert. *Commercial Law*. 6th ed. London: Sweet and Maxwell, 1987.

Osborne, Eric, Roach, Greg, and Baskind, Lee. *Commercial Law*. Oxford: Oxford University Press, 2022.

Ramlogan, Rajendra. *Commercial Law: Cases and Materials from the Commonwealth Caribbean*. St. Augustine: Rajendra Ramlogan [self-published], 2019.

Schill, Stephan W. *Yearbook Commercial Arbitration 2021*. The Hague: Wolters Kluwer, 2021.

Company Law

Burgess, Andrew D. *Commonwealth Caribbean Company Law*. Abingdon: Routledge, 2013.

Caribbean Law Institute Centre. *Bridging the Gap: A Status Report on Company Law in the CARICOM Region with Recommendations for Reform*. Bridgetown: University of the West Indies, 2016.

Ffolkes-Goldson, Suzanne C. *Corporate Business Principles: A Guide to the Jamaica Companies Act*. Kingston: Caribbean Law Publishing Company, 2020.

Mangal, Rambaran. *An Introduction to Company Law in the Commonwealth Caribbean*. Canoe Press, University of the West Indies, 2001.

Constitutional Law

Albert, Richard, O'Brien, Derek, and Wheatle, Se-shauna. *The Oxford Handbook of Caribbean Constitutions*. Oxford: Oxford University Press, 2020.

Alexis, Francis. *Changing Caribbean Constitutions*. 2nd ed. Bridgetown: Caribbean Research and Publications, 2015.

DeMerieux, Margaret. *Fundamental Rights in Commonwealth Caribbean Constitutions*. Bridgetown: Faculty of Law, University of the West Indies, 1992.

McIntosh, Simeon C. R. *Caribbean Constitutional Reform: Rethinking the West Indian Polity*. Kingston: Caribbean Law Publishing Company, 2003.

O'Brien, Derek. *The Constitutional Systems of the Commonwealth Caribbean: A Contextual Analysis*. Oxford: Hart Publishing, 2014.

Phillips, Fred. *Commonwealth Caribbean Constitutional Law*. London: Taylor and Francis, 2016.

Robinson, Tracy S., Bulkan, Arif, and Saunders, Adrian. *Fundamentals of Caribbean Constitutional Law*. 2nd ed. London: Sweet and Maxwell, 2021.

Spackman, Ann. *Constitutional Development of the West Indies: A Selection from the Major Documents*. St. Lawrence: Caribbean Universities Press, 1975.

Contract Law

Affonso, Timothy A. *Contract Law: A Commonwealth Caribbean Casebook*. XLbris, 2013.

Ashby, Lana, and O'Connor, Peter. *Simplifying Contract Law: Cases and Materials for the Commonwealth Caribbean*. Barbados: [Publisher not identified], 2014.

Chaudhary, Roop L., Cumberbatch, Jefferson O'B., and Kodilinye, Gilbert. *West Indian Law of Contract*. Heroco International Ltd., 1995.

Jackson, Nicola. *Contract Law*. 4th ed. (e-book). Oxford: Oxford University Press, 2021.

Kodilinye, Gilbert, and Kodilinye, Maria. *Commonwealth Caribbean Contract Law*. Abingdon: Routledge, 2014.

Smits, Jan M. *Contract Law: A Comparative Introduction*. 3rd ed. Cheltenham: Edward Elgar Publishing, 2021.

Criminal Law

Atkinson-Flowers, Nadine C. *On Your Feet: Criminal Law Practice in the Parish Courts in Jamaica*. Kingston: The Caribbean Law Publishing Company, 2021.

Belnavis, George. *Criminal Practice and Procedure in Magistrates' Courts in the Commonwealth Caribbean*. Kingston: Caribbean Law Publishing Company, 2009.

Loewy, Arnold H. *Criminal Law in a Nutshell*. 6th ed. St. Paul: West Academic Publishing, 2020.

Monaghan, Nicola. *Criminal Law*. 6th ed. Oxford: Oxford University Press, 2020.

Seetahal, Dana S., and Ramgoolam, Roger. *Commonwealth Caribbean Criminal Practice and Procedure*. Abingdon: Routledge, 2019.

Wilson, William. *Criminal Law*. 7th ed. Hoboken: Pearson, 2020.

Cybersecurity/Data Privacy Law

Donalds, Charlotte, Barclay, Corlane, and Osei-Bryson, Kweku-Muata. *Cybercrime and Cybersecurity in the Global South: Concepts, Strategies, and Frameworks for Greater Resilience*. Abingdon: Routledge, 2022.

Grady, Mark F., and Parisi, Francesco. *The Law and Economics of Cybersecurity*. Cambridge: Cambridge University Press, 2011.

Mireles, Michael S., and Hobaugh, Jack L., Jr. *Cybersecurity Law*. St. Paul: West Academic Publishing, 2022.

Orji, Uchenna Jerome. *Cybersecurity Law and Regulation.* Nijmegen: Wolf Legal Publishers, 2012.

Sidoni, Gabi, and Ezioni, Limor. *Cybersecurity and Legal-Regulatory Aspects.* Hackensack: World Scientific Publishing Co., 2021.

Disaster Law

Bartolini, Giulio, Cubie, Dug, Hesselman, Marlies, and Peel, Jacqueline. *Yearbook of International Disaster Law.* Leiden: Brill Nijhoff, 2020.

De Guttry, Andrea, and Gestri, Marco. *International Disaster Response Law.* The Hague: Springer, 2012.

Fitzpatrick, Daniel, and Compton, Caroline. *Law, Property and Disasters: Adaptive Perspectives from the Global South.* Abingdon: Routledge, 2021.

Giustinian, Flavia Zorzi. *International Law in Disaster Scenarios: Applicable Rules and Principles.* Cham: Springer, 2021.

Lauta, Kristian Cedervall. *Disaster Law.* Abingdon: Routledge, 2016.

Singh, Amita. *Disaster Law: Emerging Thresholds.* Abingdon: Routledge, 2018.

Drug Law

Alleyne, Desiree C. *The Law of Dangerous Drugs in the Commonwealth Caribbean: Cases and Materials.* [Place of publication not identified]:Cort's Legal Series, 2015.

Alovisetti, Charles S., and Furman, Cassia. *The Cannabis Business: Understanding Law, Finance, and Governance in America's Newest Industry.* Abingdon: Routledge, 2021.

Cohen, Barak, and Bleicher, Michael. *Cannabis Law: A Primer on Federal and State Law Regarding Marijuana, Hemp, and CDB.* Chicago: American Bar Association, 2021.

Collins, John. *Legislating the Drug Wars: A Regulatory History of U.N. Drug Control.* Cambridge: Cambridge University Press, 2022.

MacFarlane, Bruce. *Cannabis Law: The Legislative Framework*. Toronto: Thomson Reuters, 2020.

Seear, Kate. *Law, Drugs and the Making of Addiction: Just Habits*. Abingdon: Routledge, 2021.

Education Law

Anthony, Kenny. *The Legal Framework of Education in the Organisation of Eastern Caribbean States (OECS)*. Washington, DC: Organization of American States, 1994.

Chevannes, Barry. *Legislation of Tertiary Education in the Caribbean*. Caracas: International Institute for Higher Education in Latin America and the Caribbean, 2005.

Council of Legal Education: Professional Law Schools Regulations. Council of Legal Education, 2000.

Deo, Meera A., Lazarus-Black, Mindie, and Mertz, Elizabeth. *Power, Legal Education, and Law School Cultures*. Abingdon: Routledge, 2021.

Report on Survey of Legal Education in CARICOM Member States. Draft. University of the West Indies, 2017.

Employment and Labor Law

Caribbean Digest of Legislation on Termination of Employment. Port of Spain: International Labor Organization, 2008.

Corthesy, Natalie, and Harris-Roper, Carla-Anne. *Commonwealth Caribbean Employment and Labour Law*. Abingdon: Routledge, 2014.

Heckman, James J., and Pages, Carmen. *Law and Employment: Lessons from Latin America and the Caribbean*. Chicago: The University of Chicago Press, 2007.

Holland, James A., Burnett, Stuart, and Millington, Philip. *Employment Law*. Oxford: Oxford University Press, 2016.

James, Westmin R. A., and Brathwaite, Rashad. *Labour Law Guide for the Organization of Eastern Caribbean States (OECS)*. Port of Spain: International Labour Organization, 2021.

Thomas-Felix, Deborah. *Labour Law in the Commonwealth Caribbean: The Practice of Good Industrial Relations in the 21st Century*. Santa Cruz: Deborah Thomas-Felix, 2021.

Women, Labour and the Law: A Caribbean Perspective. Georgetown: International Labour Office, CARICOM, 1995.

Environmental Law

Anderson, Winston. *Principles of Caribbean Environmental Law*. Washington, DC: Environmental Law Institute, 2012.

Moss, S. G. *Environmental Legislation of the Commonwealth Caribbean*. St. Michael: Caribbean Conservation Association, 1982. (Although a bit dated, this resource is included because it is useful in researching changes in Caribbean environmental laws over time.)

O'Toole, Gavin. *Environmental Politics in Latin America and the Caribbean*. Liverpool: Liverpool University Press, 2014.

Equity and Trusts

Hudson, Alastair. *Equity and Trusts*. 10th ed. Abingdon: Routledge, 2022.

Kodilinye, Gilbert. *The Law of Trusts in the West Indies: Cases and Commentary*. 3rd ed. Cave Hill: Faculty of Law, University of the West Indies, 1993.

Kodilinye, Gilbert, and Carmichael, Trevor. *Commonwealth Caribbean Law of Trusts and Equitable Remedies*. Abingdon: Routledge-Cavendish, 2012.

Kodilinye, Gilbert, and Carmichael, Trevor. *Commonwealth Caribbean Law of Trusts*. 3rd ed. Hoboken: Taylor and Francis, 2014. (This is also in e-book format.)

Nunez-Tesheira, Karen. *Non-Contentious Probate Practice in the English-Speaking Caribbean*. Kingston: Caribbean Law Publications, 2004.

Watt, Gary. *Equity and Trusts Law*. 7th ed. Oxford: Oxford University Press, 2021.

Ethics and Obligations of the Legal Profession

Ali, Shazeeda A., Ed. *The Ethical Lawyer: A Caribbean Perspective.* London: Sweet and Maxwell, 2015.

McKoy, Derrick V. *Corruption: Law, Governance and Ethics in the Commonwealth Caribbean.* Hertford: Hansib Publications Ltd., 2012.

Nunez-Tesheira, Karen. *The Legal Profession in the English-Speaking Caribbean.* Kingston: Ian Randle Publishers, 2012.

Phillips, Fred. *Ethics of the Legal Profession.* London: Taylor and Francis, 2016.

Phillips, Fred. *Ethics in the Legal Profession: A New Order.* Abingdon: Routledge, 2012.

Sobion, Justin. *The West Indian Lawyer.* Bloomington: Balboa Press, 2020.

Family Law

Anderson, Winston. *Private International Family Law.* Kingston: Ian Randle Publishers, 2005.

Brown, Fara. *Family Law in Jamaica.* Kingston: Caribbean Law Publishing Company, 2018.

Cumper, Gloria, and Daly, Stephanie. *Family Law in the Commonwealth Caribbean.* Mona: University of the West Indies, 1979.

Daly, Stephanie. *Child and Family Law in Trinidad and Tobago.* Port of Spain: Government Printery, 1992.

Kitchin, Arthur. *Family Law and the Caribbean Family.* Women and Development Studies, Mona: University of the West Indies, 1987.

Nunez-Tesheira, Karen. *Commonwealth Caribbean Family Law: Husband, Wife and Cohabitant.* Abingdon: Routledge, 2016.

Gender and the Law

Adams, Kristine, and Byrnes, Andrew. *Gender Equality and the Judiciary: Using International Human Rights Standards to Promote the Human Rights of Women and the Girl-Child at the National Level.* London: Commonwealth Secretariat, 2000.

Beretta, Francisco. *"I Have to Leave to be Me": Discriminatory Laws Against LGBT People in the Eastern Caribbean*. New York: Human Rights Watch, 2017.

Bissessar, Ann Marie, and Huggins, Camille. *Gender and Domestic Violence in the Caribbean*. Cham: Springer, 2021.

ECLAC. *Advancing Gender Equality in the Caribbean: Legislative Approaches to Sex Discrimination*. New York: United Nations, 2001.

Ibarra, Alicia Barcena. *Gender Equality Plans in Latin America and the Caribbean: Road Maps for Development*. New York: United Nations, 2017.

LaFont, Suzanne. *The Emergence of An Afro Caribbean Legal Tradition: Gender Relations and Family Courts in Kingston, Jamaica*. San Francisco: Austin and Winfield, 1996. (Note: This is one of those unique titles straddling gender and the law, courts, family law, and legal history. It is included under this section for a tighter structure but is useful for research in all these areas and for the history and development of family courts in Jamaica.)

Stephenson, Jacqueline H., Persadie, Natalie Renee, Bissessar, Ann Marie, and Esnard, Talia. *Diversity, Equality, and Inclusion in Caribbean Organisations and Society: An Exploration of Work, Employment, Education and the Law*. Basingstoke: Palgrave Macmillan, 2021.

Human Rights

Alleyne, G. A. O., and Antoine, Rose Marie Belle. *HIV and Human Rights: Legal and Policy Perspectives on HIV and Human Rights in the Caribbean*. Mona: University of the West Indies Press, 2013.

Amnesty International. *Death Penalty in the English-Speaking Caribbean: A Human Rights Issue*. London: Amnesty International, 2012. (This is in e-book form.)

Byre, Angela D., and Byfield, Beverley Y. *International Human Rights Law in the Commonwealth Caribbean*. Dordrecht: Martinus Nijhoff, 1991.

Castaldi, Ligia De Jesus. *Abortion in Latin America and the Caribbean: The Legal Impact of the American Convention on Human Rights*. Notre Dame: University of Notre Dame Press, 2020.

Haynes, Jason. *Caribbean Anti-Trafficking Law and Practice*. Oxford: Hart Publishing, 2021.

Jayawickrama, Nihal. *The Judicial Application of Human Rights Law: National, Regional and International Jurisprudence*. Cambridge: Cambridge University Press, 2017. (The author reviewed the case law of the superior courts in 103 countries, including the Caribbean, and provides analysis of the judicial application of human rights, and the jurisprudence of institutions monitoring human rights.)

Phillips, Fred. *Death Penalties and Human Rights*. Kingston: Ian Randle Publishers Ltd., 2009.

Vasciannie, Stephen. *Caribbean Essays on Law and Policy*. Mona: University of Technology, 2020.

Wheatle, Se-shauna. *Principled Reasoning in Human Rights Adjudication*. Oxford: Hart Publishing, 2019.

Insurance Law

Arnold-Dwyer, Franziska. *Insurable Interest and the Law*. Abingdon: Routledge, 2022.

Denbow, Claude H. *Life Insurance Law in the Commonwealth Caribbean*. Hayward Heath: Tottel, 2009.

French, Christopher C., and Dobbyn, John F. *Insurance Law in a Nutshell*. 6th ed. St. Paul: West Academic Publishing, 2022.

Rego, Margarida Lima, and Kuschke, Birgit. *Insurance and Human Rights*. Cham: Springer, 2022.

Walcott, Lesley A. *Commonwealth Caribbean Insurance Law*. Abingdon: Routledge, 2019. (This is also available as an e-book.)

Intellectual Property Law

CARICOM. *Copyright and Neighbouring Rights: A Report and Model Legislation*. Georgetown: CARICOM, 1978.

Corthesy, Natalie G. S. "Brand New IP: Country Name Designation—From France With Love." In *The Future of Intellectual Property*, edited by Daniel J. Gervais. Cheltenham: Edward Elgar Publishing Limited, 2021.

Corthesy, Natalie G. S. "Country Name Designation and International IP Protection of National Competitive Identities." *Journal of Intellectual Property Law and Practice* 16, nos. 4–5 (April–May 2021): 357–67.

Corthesy, Natalie G. S. *International Intellectual Property Protection of Country Names—Balancing Nation Brands and Geographic Commons in a Competitive Global Marketplace.* Thesis. Queen Mary School of Law, University of London. [Publication date unknown].

Corthesy, Natalie G. S. "Life Plus 50: Striking a Balance Between the Term Copyright Protection and Jamaica's Public Domain." *Queen Mary Journal of Intellectual Property* 2, no. 4 (2012): 329–42.

Daley, Dianne. *IEL Intellectual Property. Jamaica Country Report.* Suppl. 47. Wolters Kluwer, 2008.

Daley, Dianne. *Institutional Issues for Developing Countries in IP Policy-Making, Administration and Enforcement: Jamaica, Trinidad & Tobago, St. Lucia.* London: Commission on Intellectual Property Rights, 2002. (This is also available as an e-book.) (Note: Dianne Daley has also written many articles on this topic as well as her dissertation, cited below.)

Daley, Dianne. *International Copyright and Developing Countries: The Impact of Recent Developments from a Jamaican Perspective.* Thesis/Dissertation. Montreal: McGill University, 1995.

Dreyfuss, Rochelle Cooper, and Pila, Justine. *The Oxford Handbook of Intellectual Property Law.* Oxford: Oxford University Press, 2018.

Jones-Hendrickson, S. B. *The Caribbean and Intellectual Property Rights.* [Place of publication unknown]: Caribbean Centre for Monetary Studies, 2000.

Kingston Mann, Larisa. *Rude Citizenship: Jamaican Popular Music, Copyright, and the Reverberations of Colonial Power*. Chapel Hill: University of North Carolina Press, 2022.

Koo, Justin. *Right of Communication to the Public in EU Copyright Law*. Oxford: Hart Publishing, 2020.

LeGall, Sharon B. *Intellectual Property, Traditional Knowledge and Cultural Property Protection: Cultural Signifiers in the Caribbean and the Americas*. Abingdon: Routledge, 2016.

United Nations Economic Commission for Latin America. Office for the Caribbean. *Patent Legislation in the CARICOM States*. Geneva: World Intellectual Property Organization, 1981. (This is useful for tracing the development of patent legislation throughout the region.)

International Law

Anderson, Winston, Ed. *Eminent Caribbean International Law Jurists: The Rule of International Law in the Caribbean*. Port of Spain: The CCJ Academy for Law, 2019.

Anderson, Winston C. *Caribbean Instruments on International Law*. Bridgetown: Winston Stone Publications, 1994.

Evans, Malcolm D. *International Law*. 5th ed. Oxford: Oxford University Press, 2018.

Odello, Marco, and Seatzu, Francesco, Eds. *Latin American and Caribbean International Institutional Law*. The Hague: T. M. C. Asser Press, 2015.

Ramcharan, B. G., and Francis, Laurel B. *Caribbean Perspectives on International Law and Organizations*. Dordrecht: MartinusNijhoff, 1989.

Shaw, Malcolm Nathan. *International Law*. 9th ed. Cambridge: Cambridge University Press, 2021.

Vasciannie, Stephen. *The International Law Workbook: Questions and Materials for Students of Public International Law*. Kingston: Stephen Vasciannie, 2016.

Van Doore, Kathryn E. *Orphanage Trafficking in International Law*. Cambridge: Cambridge University Press, 2022.

Vasciannie, Stephen. *Jamaica and the World: Aspects of International Law.* Mona: University of the West Indies, Norman Manley Law School, 2010.

Judiciary

Cooper, Jeremy. *Being a Judge in the Modern World.* Oxford: Oxford University Press, 2017.

Dakolias, Maria. *The Judicial Sector in Latin America and the Caribbean: Elements of Reform.* Washington, DC: World Bank, 1996.

The Doctrine of the Separation of Powers: The Independence of the Judiciary, the Obligation of Accountability. Ministry of the Attorney General, Trinidad and Tobago, 1999.

Ramlogan, Rajendra. *Judicial Review in the Commonwealth Caribbean.* London: Taylor and Francis, 2013.

Ryan, Selwyn D. *The Judiciary and Governance in the Caribbean.* St. Augustine: Institute of Social and Economic Studies, University of the West Indies, 2001.

Jurisprudence and Legal Theory

Dunoff, Jeffrey L., and Pollack, Mark A., Eds. *International Legal Theory: Foundations and Frontiers.* Cambridge: Cambridge University Press, 2022.

McIntosh, Simeon C. R. *Fundamental Rights and Democratic Governance: Essays in Caribbean Jurisprudence.* Kingston: Caribbean Law Publishing Company, 2005.

McIntosh, Simeon C. R. *Kelsen in the Grenada Court: Essays on Revolutionary Legality.* Kingston: Ian Randle Publishers, 2008. (This is a useful resource for researching judicial power, the Grenada Revolution, rule of law and the legitimacy of government.)

Law of the Sea/Maritime Law

Anderson, Winston. *The Law of the Sea in the Caribbean.* Leiden: Brill Nijhoff, 2022.

De Yturriaga, Jose Antonio, and Fernandez-Sanchez, Pablo Antonio. *New Approaches to the Law of the Sea*. Hauppauge: Nova Science Publishers' Inc., 2017.

International Seabed Authority. *The Law of the Sea: Compendium of Basic Documents*. Kingston: Caribbean Law Publishing Company, 2001.

Ratter, Beate M. W. *Maritime Jurisdiction in the Wider Caribbean: A Handbook on National Legislation*. Hamburg: Wayasbah, 1993.

Rothwell, Donald, Elferink, Alex G. Oude, Scott, Karen N., and Stephens, Tim. *The Oxford Handbook of the Law of the Sea*. Oxford: Oxford University Press, 2017.

Tanaka, Yoshifumi. *The International Law of the Sea*. Cambridge: Cambridge University Press, 2019.

Vasciannie, Stephen C. *Land-Locked and Geographically Disadvantaged States in the International Law of the Sea*. Oxford: Clarendon Press, 2001.

Legal Drafting and Interpretation

Bennion, Francis Alan Roscoe. *Understanding Common Law Legislation: Drafting and Interpretation*. Oxford: Oxford University Press, 2009.

Borda, Aldo Zammit. *Legislative Drafting*. Abingdon: Routledge, 2015.

Butt, Peter. *Modern Legal Drafting: A Guide to Using Clearer Language*. 3rd ed. Cambridge: Cambridge University Press, 2018.

Crabbe, V. C. R. A. C. *Crabbe on Legislative Drafting*. 2nd ed. Durban: LexisNexis, 2008.

Emmet, David. *Drafting*. Oxford: Oxford University Press, 2020.

Fandl, Kevin. J. *Lost in Translation: Effective Legal Writing for the International Legal Community*. New Providence: LexisNexis, 2013.

Kuney, George W., and Looper, Donna C. *Legal Drafting in a Nutshell*. St. Paul: West Academic Publishing, 2021.

Salembier, Paul. *Legal and Legislative Drafting*. Toronto: LexisNexis, 2018.

Xanthaki, Helen. *Enhancing Legislative Drafting in the Commonwealth: A Wealth of Innovation*. London: Routledge, 2020.

Legal History

Collins, Justine K. *Tracing British West Indian Slavery Laws: A Comparative Analysis of Legal Transplants*. Abingdon: Routledge, 2022.

Sandberg, Russell. *Subversive Legal History: A Manifesto for the Future of Legal Education*. Abingdon: Routledge, 2021.

Tomlins, Christopher, and Boalt, Elizabeth Josselyn. *Comparative Legal History*. Cheltenham: Edward Elgar Publishing, 2021.

Private International Law

Anderson, Winston. *Caribbean Private International Law*. London: Sweet and Maxwell, 2014.

Anderson, Winston. *Elements of Private International Law*. Kingston: Caribbean Law Publishing Company, 2003.

Hay, Peter. *Advanced Introduction to Private International Law and Procedure*. Cheltenham: Edward Elgar Publishing, 2018.

Symeonides, Symeon. *Private International Law: Idealism, Pragmatism, Eclecticism*. Leiden: Brill Nijhoff, 2021.

Property Law/Land Law

Carmichael, Trevor A., and Mahon, Susan D. *Land Use Under the Law: A Commentary and Compilation of Select Legislation in Small Island Developing States*. Kingston: Caribbean Law Publications, 1994. (Note: though this is a bit dated, it is useful for a history of legislation relating to land law.)

Kodilinye, Gilbert. *Commonwealth Caribbean Property Law*. 5th ed. Abingdon: Routledge, 2022.

Lim, Hilary, and Home, Robert K. *Demystifying the Mystery of the Capital: Land Tenure and Poverty in Africa and the Caribbean*. London: Glasshouse Press, 2004.

Owusu, Sampson. *Commonwealth Caribbean Land Law*. London: Routledge-Cavendish, 2015.

Public Law

Brown, Lionel Neville. *Legal Education and Public Law: Report on a Commonwealth Foundation Caribbean Lecture Tour, December 1975–January 1976)*. London: The Foundation, 1976.

Elliott, Mark, and Thomas, Robert. *Public Law*. 4th ed. Oxford University Press.

Faragher, Colin. *Public Law*. 7th ed. Oxford: Oxford University Press, 2021.

Fiadjoe, Albert K. *Commonwealth Caribbean Public Law*. Abingdon: Routledge, 2015. (This is also available in e-book format.)

Vasciannie, Stephen. *Arguments and Facts: Caribbean Public Law, Governance, Economy, and Society*. Kingston: New Caribbean Publishers, 2016.

Reparatory Justice

Beckles, Hilary. *Britain's Black Debt: Reparations for Caribbean Slavery and Native Genocide*. Kingston: University of the West Indies Press, 2013.

Beckles, Hilary. *How Britain Underdeveloped the Caribbean: A Reparation Response to Europe's Legacy of Plunder and Poverty*. Kingston: University of the West Indies Press, 2021.

Buser, Andreas. *Colonial Injustices and the Law of State Responsibility: The CARICOM Claim for Reparations*. Berlin: Potsdam University, 2017. (This is also available in e-book format.)

Gonsalves, Ralph E. *The Case for Caribbean Reparatory Justice: Four Essays*. [Place of publication unknown]: Strategy Forum Inc., 2014.

Hira, Sandew. *20 Questions and Answers on Reparations for Colonialism*. The Hague: Amrit Publishers, 2014.

Leibowitz, Arnold H. *Colonial Emancipation in the Pacific and the Caribbean: A Legal and Political Analysis*. New York: Praeger, 1976.

Sports Law

Anderson, Paul M., Blackshaw, Ian S., Siekmann, Robert C. R., and Soek, Janwillem. *Sports Betting Law and Policy*. The Hague: Springer, 2012.

Beloff, Michael Jacob, Kerr, Tim, Demetriou, Marie, and Beloff, Rupert. *Sports Law*. 3rd ed. Oxford: Hart Publishing, 2017.

Haynes, Jason, and Marcus, J. Tyrone. *Commonwealth Caribbean Sports Law*. Abingdon: Routledge, 2019.

James, Mark. *Sports Law*. Basingstoke: Palgrave, 2017.

Thorpe, David, Buti, Antonio, Davies, Chris, and Jonson, Paul. *Sports Law*. 3rd ed. Oxford: Oxford University Press, 2017.

Tax Law

Amos, Jude, and DeBrauw-Hay, Elizabeth. *Taxation and Investment in the Caribbean*. Amsterdam: International Bureau of Fiscal Documentation, 2007. (Coverage started in 1991 and was last updated in 2007.)

Campbell, Aretha M. *Money Laundering, Terrorist Financing, and Tax Evasion: The Consequences of International Policy Initiatives on Financial Centres in the Caribbean Region*. Basingstoke: Palgrave Macmillan, 2021.

Denbow, Claude H. *Income Tax Law in the Commonwealth Caribbean*. Haywards Heath: Bloomsbury Professional, 2013.

Tort Law

Deakin, S. F., and Adams, Zoe. *Markesinis and Deakin's Tort Law*. 8th ed. Oxford: Oxford University Press, 2019.

Horsey, Kristy, and Rackley, Erica. *Tort Law*. 7th ed. Oxford: Oxford University Press, 2021.

Hughes-Davies, Timon, and Tamblyn, Nathan. *Tort Law*. Abingdon: Routledge, 2020.

Kodilinye, Gilbert. *Caribbean Tort Law*. London: Cavendish, 2003.

Kodilinye, Gilbert, Anderson, Roy, and Kodilinye, Vanessa. *Commonwealth Caribbean Tort Law*. 6th ed. Abingdon: Routledge, 2022.

Digests and Reports

The Barbados Law Reports. Family Law Cases 1982–2007. Office of the Attorney General, 2013.

British West Indian Cases. Index. Faculty of Law, University of the West Indies, Cave Hill, January–December 1976. (After June 2021, no further editions or updates were located on WorldCat.)

The Caribbean Commercial Law Reports. Law Institute, University of the West Indies, Cave Hill, 1991.

Caribbean Criminal Law Digest. Caribbean Law Publishing in Association with Council for Legal Education, Norman Manley Law School. (Coverage is from 2010 onward.)

Caribbean Digest of Legislation on Termination of Employment. International Labor Organization, 2008.

The Eastern Caribbean Law Reports. Caribbean Law Publishing Company, 2003.

Encyclopedias

With respect to encyclopedias on Caribbean law, several searches on WorldCat during the preparation of this book only yielded the following, which, though a bit dated, might still be useful:

Redden, Kenneth Robert, and Schlueter, Linda L. *Modern Legal Systems Encyclopedia. Central America and the Caribbean.* Hein, 1989.

Law Journals

The Caribbean Journal of Legal Information: Bulletin of the Caribbean Association of Law Librarians. 1987.

Caribbean Labour Journal. LabCom International, 1991. (Also available in electronic format.)

The Caribbean Law Review. Faculty of Law, University of the West Indies. 1991. (This is also available in electronic format.)

Latin American and Caribbean Journal of Legal Studies. Berkeley Electronic Press. Coverage is from 2006 onwards.

Chapter 10

Researching Treaties and Regional and International Organizations

This chapter provides an overview of treaty research and will discuss the legal resources of regional and international organizations. It provides links to United States Congressional documents relating to treaties, research guides on treaty research, and general texts on the topic.

What Is a Treaty?

A treaty is a negotiated agreement between two or more states. Other terms for treaties are conventions, charters, agreements, protocols, or accords. Treaties can be bilateral (between two countries) or multilateral (involving multiple states or international organizations). For validity, a treaty requires formal signing by authorized state representatives. The ratification process is where the state's own requirements and procedures are followed, and notification and consent to the other state parties that are to be bound by the terms of the treaty.

Travaux preparatoires (preparatory documents) are the documents that arose out of the discussions, negotiations, and the drafting of the final text of a treaty. They are, therefore, important in

Figure 3 The Treaty-Making Process

providing a greater understanding of the details involved in the drafting and negotiating history of treaties. Figure 3 highlights the treaty-making process.

Caribbean regional integration has led to several important treaties. Treaty-making is also an ongoing process. Treaty research skills are, therefore, important, and there are many resources for finding bilateral and multilateral treaties. Following this section, a useful bibliography has been included with respect to researching international treaties and agreements generally, but also treaty-making in the Caribbean.

The Association of Caribbean States

The Association of Caribbean States (ACS) is a group of approximately thirty-six Caribbean states that was formed to improve cooperation based on their proximity and historical ties. Of the thirty-six states, twenty-five are members, three are associate members, and eight are nonindependent states that are eligible for associate membership. The Convention Establishing the ACS (http://www.acs-aec.org/index.php?q=about/convention-establishing-the-association-of-caribbean-states, accessed May 30, 2022) was signed on July 24, 1994, in Colombia.

There are five special committees that focus on the following:

- Trade Development and External Economic Relations;
- Sustainable Tourism;
- Transport;
- Disaster Risk Reduction; and
- Budget and Administration.

The Library General Secretariat (http://www.acs-aec.org/index.php?q=resources/library/generalsecretariat, accessed May 30, 2022) link provides access to many legal instruments of the ACS. These include Ministerial Agreements, Declarations, Plan of Action, Meeting Reports, and Summit documents.

The Caribbean Community (CARICOM)

The Caribbean Community (CARICOM), headquartered in Georgetown, Guyana, is a group of twenty states. Fifteen of these states have member status, while five are associates, and eight have observer status. CARICOM was established on July 4, 1973, with the signing of the Treaty of Chaguaramas by the prime ministers of Barbados, Guyana, Jamaica, and Trinidad and Tobago. Prior to CARICOM, the region operated under the Caribbean Free Trade Association (CARIFTA), which was established in 1968. In 2002, the Treaty of Chaguaramas was revised to allow for the establishment of the Caribbean Single Market and Economy.

The mandate of the CARICOM Secretariat is to "contribute, in support of Member States, to the improvement of the quality of life of the People of the Community and the development of an innovative and productive society in partnership with institutions and groups working towards attaining a people-centred, sustainable and internationally competitive Community" (CARICOM website, https://caricom.org/ accessed January 1, 2021).

The following are useful documents for researching CARICOM:

- CARICOM Secretariat Treaties Database (https://caricom.org/treaties/, accessed May 30, 2022)
- Revised Treaty of Chaguaramas 2002 (https://treaty.caricom.org/, accessed May 30, 2022)
- Community Decisions (https://caricom.org/community-decisions/, accessed May 30, 2022)

The Caribbean Court of Justice

Inaugurated on April 16, 2005, the Caribbean Court of Justice (CCJ), is located in Port of Spain, Trinidad and Tobago. The court was established with the expectation that it will serve as a court of last resort for Caribbean states, eventually replacing the Judicial Committee of the Privy Council in the United Kingdom.

The Agreement Establishing the CCJ entered into force on July 23, 2002. The following twelve countries are signatories to the agreement: Antigua and Barbuda; Barbados; Belize; Dominica; Grenada; Guyana; Jamaica; St. Kitts and Nevis; St. Lucia; St. Vincent and the Grenadines; Suriname; and Trinidad and Tobago. To date, only Barbados and Guyana have made the court their final appellate court.

The court has dual jurisdictions: appellate and original. The original jurisdiction (Part 11, Article X1) pertains to the interpretation and application of the Treaty Establishing the Caribbean Community. With respect to its appellate jurisdiction, the court will review and rule on appeals arising from civil and criminal cases originating from common law courts in the jurisdiction of states party to the Agreement Establishing the Caribbean Court of Justice.

Organization of American States

The Organization of American States (OAS) is the oldest regional organization in the world. The headquarters are in Washington, DC, and there are currently thirty-five member states. The genesis of the OAS dates back to the holding of the First International Conference of American States in Washington, DC, from October 1889 to April 1890. At that conference, the International Union of American Republics was approved. This event paved the way for the drafting and signing of the Charter of the OAS (http://www.oas.org/en/sla/dil/inter_american_treaties_A-41_charter_OAS.asp, accessed May 30, 2022) in 1948, which entered into force in December 1951. The Charter has since had the following amendments.

- Protocol of Buenos Aires (http://www.oas.org/dil/treaties_B-31_Protocol_of_Buenos_Aires_sign.htm, accessed May 30, 2022). Signed in 1967 and entered into force in February 1970.
- Protocol of Cartagena de Indias (http://www.oas.org/dil/treaties_A-50_Protocol_of_Cartagena_de_Indias_sign.htm, accessed May 30, 2022). Signed in 1985 and entered into force in November 1988.
- Protocol of Managua (http://www.oas.org/dil/treaties_A-58_Protocol_of_Managua_sign.htm, accessed May 30, 2022). Signed in 1993 and entered into force in January 1996.
- Protocol of Washington (http://www.oas.org/dil/treaties_A-56_Protocol_of_Washington_sign.htm, accessed May 30, 2022). Signed in 1992 and entered into force in September 1997.

The OAS has a wealth of resources for treaty research, and these are outlined below:

- Overview of Treaty Agreements (https://www.oas.org/en/sla/dil/treaties_agreements.asp, accessed May 30, 2022)

- Multilateral Treaties (https://www.oas.org/en/sla/dil/inter_american_treaties.asp, accessed May 30, 2022). Here, you can search by either year of the treaty or the subject. There are also options to search by member states or by convention.
- Bilateral Agreements (https://www.oas.org/en/sla/dil/bilateral_agreements.asp, accessed May 30, 2022). This link allows for searching alphabetically, with coverage from 1949 to 2020. Alternatively, searching can be done by year, covering 2003–2020.

Organisation of Eastern Caribbean States (OECS)

The Treaty of Basseterre established the Organisation of Eastern Caribbean States (OECS) and was signed on June 18, 1981, by Antigua and Barbuda, Dominica, Grenada, Montserrat, St. Kitts and Nevis, St. Lucia, and St. Vincent and the Grenadines.

The Revised Treaty of Basseterre (https://www.govt.lc/treaty-of-basseterre, accessed May 30, 2022) was signed on June 18, 2010, and established the OECS Economic Union.

United Nations Systems Treaty Research Sources

The United Nations is perhaps one of the best resources for treaty research. Article 102 of the Charter of the United Nations requires "Every treaty and every international agreement entered into by any Member of the United Nations after the present Charter comes into force shall as soon as possible be registered with the Secretariat and published by it" (United Nations website, https://www.un.org/en accessed February 14, 2022). To date, approximately 560 multilateral treaties on a variety of subjects have been deposited with the secretary-general of the United Nations.

Listed below are some of the important United Nations resources for locating treaties.

- Dag Hammarskjold Library (https://www.un.org/en/library/page/un-resources-documents, accessed May 30, 2022). The Dag Hammarskjold Library of the United Nations contains treaties, resolutions, speeches, maps, yearbooks, research guides, and other data. It also has an oral history collection. There is a helpful Thesaurus (https://metadata.un.org/thesaurus/?lang=en, accessed May 30, 2022), and the library facilitates searching by document type, or by a specific United Nations body or its agencies.
- United Nations Treaty Collection (https://treaties.un.org/, accessed May 30, 2022).

The UN Treaty Collection provides information on:

- The Status of Treaties Deposited with the Secretary-General (https://treaties.un.org/Pages/ParticipationStatus.aspx?clang=_en, accessed May 30, 2022). There are twenty-nine chapters covering a variety of topics.
- United Nations Treaty Collection (https://treaties.un.org/Pages/AdvanceSearch.aspx?tab=UNTS&clang=_en, accessed May 30, 2022). The United Nations Treaty Collection database can be searched by volume, title, or participant. The database's Cumulative Index (https://treaties.un.org/Pages/CumulativeIndexes.aspx?clang=_en, accessed May 30, 2022) also facilitates searching through registration periods. This collection also has a useful Treaty Event tab for searching current, past, and special treaty events. The Titles of Multilateral Treaties (https://treaties.un.org/pages/Content.aspx?path=DB/titles/page1_en.xml, accessed May 30, 2022) is available in the six official languages of the United Nations and is helpful if you know the actual title of the treaty you want to access.

The United Nations Treaty Collection has additional resources under its Resources tab, and these include the Treaty Handbook, Model Instruments, Regulations, and Notes Verbales.

- League of Nations Treaties (https://treaties.un.org/Pages/LON.aspx?clang=_en, accessed May 30, 2022). These are useful for researching pre-United Nations agreements, dating as far back as 1921.

Tracing the History of Treaties or Finding the *Travaux preparatoires*

Travaux preparatoires is the term for all the associated drafting documents, negotiations, and other preparatory documents leading up to the completion of the treaty. They are helpful in providing the treaty context, key players, and important supplementary information. Below are some helpful sources for locating these documents:

- New York University Law Library Guide (https://nyulaw.libguides.com/c.php?g=773832&p=5551920, accessed May 30, 2022): Commentaries and *travaux preparatoires* (drafting history)
- Globalex (https://www.nyulawglobal.org/globalex/Travaux_Preparatoires1.html, accessed May 30, 2022): An approach to researching the drafting history of international agreements
- United Nations' Diplomatic Conferences (https://legal.un.org/diplomaticconferences/, accessed May 30, 2022): Coverage from 1958 to 1998
- International Law Commission (https://legal.un.org/ilc/ilcintro.shtml, accessed May 30, 2022): Analytical guide to the work of the international law commission

- The Yearbook of the United Nations (https://www.un.org/yearbook, accessed May 30, 2022): This is an extensive collection of yearbooks spanning 1946 to 2014. There is a general search box, or a specific yearbook can be selected for download.
- The Audiovisual Library of International Law (https://legal.un.org/avl/intro/introduction.html?tab=2, accessed May 30, 2022): This library also has a Historic Archives (https://legal.un.org/avl/historicarchives.html, accessed September 20, 2023) section for locating *Travaux preparatoires.*

Other General Online Treaty Research Sources

- Congress.Gov Treaty Documents (https://www.congress.gov/search?q=%7B%22source%22:%22treaties%22%7D&-searchResultViewType=expanded, accessed May 30, 2022). This site monitors treaties via the Senate. Treaty documents are available since the 94th Congress (1975–1976). Treaties that were pending in 1975 are included. The United States Senate Committee on Foreign Relations (https://www.foreign.senate.gov/#sfrc, accessed May 30, 2022) is also useful for researching hearings and activities and accessing reports. Here, you can review pending treaties (https://www.foreign.senate.gov/treaties, accessed May 30, 2022) that have been referred to the committee.
- Georgetown University Law Library Treaty Research Guide (https://guides.ll.georgetown.edu/TreatyResearch, accessed May 30, 2022).
- Globalex: An Introduction to Sources for Treaty Research (https://www.nyulawglobal.org/globalex/Treaty_Research.html, accessed May 30, 2022).

International Regional Organizations

African Union

(https://au.int/, accessed May 26, 2022)

In July 2002, the African Union (AU) replaced the former Organisation of African Unity (1963–1999). It is made up of fifty-five member states from five geographic regions (Central, Eastern, Northern, Southern, and Western) in Africa.

The vision of the AU is "An Integrated, Prosperous and Peaceful Africa, driven by its own citizens and representing a dynamic force in the global arena." An expanded version can be found in the Constitutive Act of the African Union (https://au.int/en/treaties/constitutive-act-african-union) and the Protocol on Amendments to the Constitutive Act of the African Union (https://au.int/treaties/protocol-amendments-constitutive-act-african-union, both accessed May 26, 2022).

In a bid to transform the region, the AU set up Agenda 2063, which is a blueprint and plan for the next fifty years. It includes plans focusing on "social and economic development, continental and regional integration, democratic governance and peace and security."

The AU structure is made of the following organs:

- Assembly of Heads of States and Governments
- Executive Council
- Permanent Representatives Committee
- Peace and Security Council
- Specialised Technical Committees
- AU Commission
- New Partnership for Africa's Development Agency (NEPAD)
- African Continental Free Trade Area (AfCTA) (https://au-afcfta.org/about/, accessed May 26, 2022).

- Pan-African Parliament
- Economic, Social and Cultural Council
- African Commission on Human and People's Rights
- African Court on Human and Peoples' Rights

All information about this organization, especially treaties, is available on their website. Case law of cases heard before the African Court on Human and People's Rights are available on the court's website, while selected ones are reported on the Oxford Reports on International Law database.

Economic Community of West African States

(https://ecowas.int/, accessed May 26, 2022)

The Economic Community of West African States (ECOWAS) was established for the purpose of integrating a region with similar cultural, economic, and political history. The organization is made up of fifteen member states located in West Africa, namely: Republic of Benin, Burkina Faso, Cape Verde, Côte d'Ivoire, The Gambia, Ghana, Guinea, Guinea Bissau, Liberia, Mali, Niger, Nigeria, Senegal, Sierra Leone, and Togo.

ECOWAS was formally constituted by the treaty signed by member states in 1975 in Lagos, Nigeria. The current revised treaty (https://www.ecowas.int/wp-content/uploads/2015/01/Revised-treaty.pdf, accessed May 26, 2022) was signed in Cotonou, Benin Republic, in July 1992 as a result of new developments and mandates for the Community. It contains the fundamental principles and guides its objectives of promoting economic cooperation and regional integration.

ECOWAS functions under the following institutions as well as numerous specialized agencies:

- ECOWAS Commission
- Community Court of Justice
- Community Parliament

- ECOWAS Bank for Investment and Development
- West African Health Organisation
- The Inter-Governmental Action Group against Money Laundering and Terrorism Financing in West Africa

One of the milestones and achievements of the organization is the implementation and launch of a convertible currency among member states as well as the launch of the ECOWAS passport for movement of citizens. Information about the Community, especially cases, practice directions, and laws of the Community Court of Justice, are available on the website.

Southern African Development Community

(https://www.sadc.int/, accessed May 26, 2022)

The origins of the Southern African Development Community (SADC) date back to the signing of the Lusaka Declaration in 1979 by nine southern African nations under the auspices of the Southern Africa Development Coordination Conference (SADCC), which was later inaugurated in 1980.

Due to the many political developments in the region, the SADCC was changed to SADC on August 17, 1992, when the SADC Declaration and Treaty https://www.sadc.int/sites/default/files/2021-11/Declaration__Treaty_of_SADC_0.pdf, accessed September 20, 2023) was signed. This implied that it moved from being a conference to a community of states.

Currently, the SADC is made up of the following sixteen member states: Angola, Botswana, Comoros, Democratic Republic of Congo, Eswatini, Lesotho, Madagascar, Malawi, Mauritius, Mozambique, Namibia, Seychelles, South Africa, Tanzania, Zambia, and Zimbabwe.

The mission of the organization is "to promote sustainable and equitable economic growth and socioeconomic development through efficient, productive systems, deeper cooperation and integration, good governance, and durable peace and security; so that the region emerges as a competitive and effective player in international relations and the world economy."

The SADC is made up the following institutions that are responsible for managing its operations:

- Summit of Heads or State or Government
- Summit Troika of the Organ
- SADC Tribunal
- SADC Council of Ministers
- Sectoral and Cluster Ministerial Committees
- Standing Committee of Senior Officials
- SADC Secretariat
- SADC National Committees
- SADC Parliamentary Forum

References

Amao, Olufemi. *African Union law: The Emergence of a Sui Generis Legal Order*. London; New York: Routledge Taylor and Francis Group, 2019.

Anderson, Winston. "Treaty Making in Caribbean Law and Practice: The Question of Parliamentary Participation." *Caribbean Law Review*: vol. 8, 75–115. 1988

Aust, Anthony. *Modern Treaty Law and Practice*. 3rd ed. Cambridge: Cambridge University Press, 2014.

Bernal, Richard L. *Globalization, Trade, and Economic Development: A Study of the CARIFORUM-EU Economic Partnership Agreement*. Basingstoke: Palgrave MacMillan, 2013.

Berry, David S. *Caribbean Integration Law*. Oxford: Oxford University Press, 2014. (This resource provides an analysis of current treaties and rules relating to CARICOM and the OECS.)

Blackstone's EU Treaties and Legislation, 2019–2020. 30th ed. Oxford: Oxford University Press, 2019.

Calamita, N. Jansen, and Sattorova, Mavluda. *The Regionalization of International Investment Treaty Arrangements*. London: British Institute of International and Comparative Law, 2015. (There is a chapter on regional investment treaty arrangements in the Caribbean.)

Fassbender, Bardo, Peters, Anne, Peter, Simone, and Hogger, Daniel. *The Oxford Handbook of the History of International Law*. Oxford: Oxford University Press, 2014.

Gardiner, Richard K. *Treaty Interpretation*. 2nd ed. Oxford: Oxford University Press, 2017.

Grosek, Edward. "How to Research International Treaties and Agreements." *Loyola of Los Angeles International and Comparative Law Review* (1998): 1–87. https://digitalcommons.lmu.edu/cgi/viewcontent.cgi?article=1451&context=ilr (accessed May 26, 2022).

Hollis, Duncan B. *The Oxford Guide to Treaties*. Oxford: Oxford University Press, 2020.

Kavass's Current Treaty Index. S. Hein & Company, 2008. (Note: This is a continually updated resource. It is available through HeinOnline.)

Looney, Robert, and Sparks, Donald. *Handbook of International Trade Agreements: Country, Regional and Global Approaches*. New York: Routledge, 2018.

Robinson, Patrick, Walker, Michelle, Thompson, Gerald, and Murdoch, Colin. *Manual on Treaty Law, Negotiation and Drafting for Caribbean Professionals*. Bridgetown: Caribbean Law Institute Centre, 2019.

Treaty Research. Georgetown University Law Library Research Guide. https://guides.ll.georgetown.edu/TreatyResearch (accessed May 26, 2022).

United Nations Office for Disarmament Affairs. *Disarmament and Related Treaties*. New York: United Nations, 2015.

Chapter 11

Foreign, Comparative, and International Law Research

The global state of the world often requires the knowledge of foreign, comparative, and international law. It is important to understand the legal systems of different jurisdictions as well as knowing how to locate and find the laws. This chapter discusses what to expect when researching foreign, comparative, and international law, and where to find and locate materials. It identifies the different legal citation styles that are used in some of the jurisdictions covered. Professional associations have an important role to play in the work of researchers from different jurisdictions; they bring them together for professional development activities. This chapter discusses and identifies some of these groups.

What Is Foreign Law?

Foreign law is the local and domestic law of a country. Foreign law is also referred to as national law. It is enforceable only as an internal instrument and has no impact outside that jurisdiction. Examples of foreign law include constitutions, statutes, regulations, and court decisions.

When researching foreign law, it is important to understand that various languages may exist in different jurisdictions; as a result, one must envision that there will be an official language outside of the known and common ones such as English, French, Spanish, and Portuguese. It is a common practice for librarians working as foreign, comparative, and international law experts to understand how to read, write, and speak a foreign language in addition to English.

Using an official authorized translator if you're trying to translate a document from its original language is very good practice. It is now common for most official websites to have a translation for other languages if the material resides online.

Understanding the different legal systems of the world when researching foreign law is required. Juriglobe (http://www.juriglobe.ca/eng/, accessed May 26, 2022, and August 19, 2023) gives a visual and graphic illustration of legal systems of the world with examples.

- Common law system
- Civil law system
- Customary legal system
- Religious legal system
- Mixed legal system

It is always helpful to have a broad understanding of the existing legal institutions in a jurisdiction when researching foreign law. For example, knowing about the hierarchy of courts and the judicial system of the country you're researching is very important. This will help you navigate how and where to find foreign law materials. Reading about the history, culture, and society of the jurisdiction you are researching helps broaden your knowledge and understanding. This kind of information can be found in publications such as *World Factbook*, encyclopedias, and research guides. The Globalex foreign law research guides are a leading example of publications where you find information about foreign jurisdictions. It provides access to legal information of over 150 countries around the world. Some of the guides are written by experts who are originally from these countries or are experts on the legal system.

The *Foreign Law Guide* is a compilation of legal information of 190 jurisdictions. The information found in this database include the sources of legal information and court systems, and English translations of selected foreign materials and secondary resources. This online resource contains valuable information about these jurisdictions and is updated periodically to reflect any changes about government, judicial, and court systems.

The Law Library of Congress has published very useful research guides on foreign law covering many parts of the world. *The Guide to Law Online: Nations of the World* covers sixty-five nations and has extensive coverage and information about legal resources. The online catalogue is extremely useful because the Library of Congress collects, acquires, and receives publications from all over the world. These leading publications are very useful for researchers working on smaller jurisdictions as well as emerging nations where it may be very challenging to find their information online.

WorldLII is available freely on the internet and provides access to selected legal information for over 150 jurisdictions. The information includes constitutions, case law, legislation, codes, and secondary materials such as journal articles. This website is especially useful for locating information for smaller jurisdictions and, in some instances, English translation of documents where English is not the official language.

What Is Comparative Law?

Comparative law is a concept that covers the whole range of jurisdictions, topics, and legal systems. It is not limited to the foreign law of a particular jurisdiction. Hoffman and Rumsey (2012, p. 160) noted that "Beyond comparing legal systems or jurisdictions, many comparative works focus on specific laws, topics, or regional comparisons." For example, comparative law covers all the topics in law such as contracts, commercial transactions, business law, torts, criminal law, etc. This denotes the way in which different jurisdictions function, aligning with their legal systems.

Bhat (2020, p. 267) describes comparative legal research as "the comparative evaluation of human experience occurring in the legal domains of different situations and jurisdictions." He noted that this experience widens and exposes the researcher's understanding of law and legal systems.

Winer et al. (2013, p. 16) described comparative law as "an academic study of comparing different national legal systems or parts of them, against each other." For example, comparative law research can look at the civil legal systems of two different countries such as Spain and China.

Because comparative law spreads across all the areas of law, an effective search begins with secondary resources such as encyclopedias, research guides, books, and journals. There are multitudes of materials comparing different aspects of law from one jurisdiction to another.

What Is International Law?

International law is what brings nations of the world and people together. It has evolved over the years, changing and adapting to new content and situations. International law is one of the sources of law in many legal systems. For the purpose of legal research, it is important and fundamental to understand the distinction between two areas of international law—public and private international law.

Public international law traditionally involves legal matters between different countries referred to as "states." It has evolved over the years to include issues and disputes between international organizations, private companies, and individuals. Doebbler (2018, p. 331) in his definition of international law affirmed that it is "based on states' consent or consensus, although individuals and non-state actors are increasingly having an influence on the creation of this law."

Private international law, also referred to as conflict of laws, is the interpretation of laws when legal issues arise among individuals and companies engaged in international activities. Fox (1997, p. 255) defines it as the "rules which govern the choice of law in private matters." Private international law is applicable to matters related to domicile, contract, damages, and marriage, among others. Treaties and conventions are implemented to resolve disputes.

Researchers of international law must consult the works of publicists and scholarly authorities who have published works that will give fundamental understanding of various concepts, ideologies, and terminologies. This aligns with Article 38(d) of the Statute of International Court of Justice, which states that:

> The Court, whose function is to decide in accordance with international law such disputes as are submitted to it, shall apply: . . . subject to the provisions of Article 59, judicial decisions and the teachings of the most highly qualified publicists of the various nations, as subsidiary means for the determination of rules of law.

Hoffman and Rumsey (2012) noted that publicists can be identified by the number of publications and how often they are cited. These are experts who were pioneers in proposing some underlying theories of international law. Some of them have been tasked with creating and starting the work of many international organizations.

The following are examples of subscription databases for researching international law:

- *Brill Online*: This database contains books, yearbooks, and journals on international law, human rights, and humanitarian law.
- *HeinOnline Foreign and International Law Resources Database*: This database has a series of materials covering international law such as yearbooks of international organizations, publications of the American Society of International Law, international tribunals, and judicial decisions.

- *Oxford Scholarly Authorities on International Law*: A database of e-books also available in print published by experts in all areas of international law.
- *Max Planck Encyclopaedia of International Law*: A database of articles on different areas of international law. It also includes entries with definitions of concepts and terminologies.

Legal Citation

Legal citation is an important step in legal research and writing. It is important for a researcher to understand how to cite foreign materials as well as international law documents such as treaties. There will be occasions when researchers may need to submit articles to international journals and will be required to use different citation styles. For example, if submitting to an Australian law journal, there is the likelihood that the preferred style will be the *Australian Guide to Legal Citation*. Each jurisdiction tends to have their own citation style with sections on how to style domestic, foreign, and international law materials. Some of these citation styles are available electronically on the internet or by subscription as well as in print formats.

- *Australia Guide to Legal Citation*, 4th edition (https://law.unimelb.edu.au/__data/assets/pdf_file/0005/3181325/AGLC4-with-Bookmarks-1.pdf, accessed May 26, 2022): A publication of the Melbourne University Law Review Association Inc. in collaboration with the Melbourne Journal of International Law Inc.
- *The Bluebook: A Uniform System of Citation*, 21st edition: Compiled by the editors of the *Columbia Law Review*, the *Harvard Law Review*, the *University of Pennsylvania Law Review*, and the *Yale Law Journal*.

- *Canadian Guide to Uniform Legal Citation*, 9th edition: This guide, also known as the "McGill Guide," is compiled by the editorial team of the *McGill Law Journal* and has been adopted by many Canadian law journals. It is available electronically by subscription on Westlaw Edge Canada, while the print edition is published by Thomson Reuters.
- *The Maroonbook: The University of Chicago Manual of Legal Citation Volume 87* , https://lawreview.uchicago.edu/about/view-maroonbook (accessed September 29, 2023): This citation style was compiled by the editorial team of the *University of Chicago Law Review*. It is their official citation guide, but it is being used by other journals.
- *Oxford Standards for Citation of Legal Authorities* (OSCOLA), 4th edition (https://www.law.ox.ac.uk/sites/files/oxlaw/oscola_4th_edn_hart_2012.pdf, accessed May 26, 2022): A publication of the Faculty of Law, University of Oxford.
- *OSCOLA Ireland*, 2nd edition (http://legalcitation.ie/wp-content/uploads/2016/04/OSCOLA-Ireland-2016.pdf, accessed May 26, 2022): This is an amended version of *OSCOLA UK* to cite legal materials for Ireland.

Locating Foreign and Comparative Law Materials

There are many print and electronic resources available for finding and locating foreign and comparative law materials. As mentioned earlier in this chapter, Globalex, *Foreign Law Guide*, *The Guide to Law Online: Nations of the World*, and WorldLII are good starting points for researching foreign law.

This section has identified selected jurisdictions by the type of legal system with some suggested resources, mostly commercial, for locating materials. Foreign law researchers should consult research guides published by professional librarians in law schools in these jurisdictions; they are regularly updated with useful information and a list of resources.

Common Law Jurisdictions

Australia

Australasian Legal Information Institute (http://www.austlii.edu.au/, accessed May 26, 2022): Australasian Legal Information Institute (AustLII) is a free database available on the internet. It provides access to case law, legislation, treaties, and journal articles covering Australian states, territories, and New Zealand. It provides comprehensive coverage in addition to print materials and subscriptions in online databases.

Informit is a subscription-based database that provides access to over five hundred and sixty Australian journals covering different legal topics.

LexisNexis Australia: This database provides access to books, practice materials, case law, legislation, journals, legal encyclopedias, and current awareness materials.

Thomson Reuters Australia: The products available on Thomson Reuters Australia include Westlaw, Practical Law, which provide access to books, practice materials, case law, legislation, journals, and current awareness materials.

Canada

Canadian Legal Information Institute (https://www.canlii.org/en/, accessed May 26, 2022): Canadian Legal Information Institute (CanLII) is a free database containing cases from all levels of courts and legislation from federal, province, and territory levels. There are materials from selected administrative tribunals. Now its coverage includes case commentaries and summaries, law journals, and selected e-books.

HeinOnline: One of the databases in HeinOnline provides full text access to statutes for federal, provincial, and territorial laws of

Canada, Supreme Court of Canada Reports, and the Revised Statutes of Canada.

Lexis Advance Quicklaw: This database provides access to Canadian case law (from courts and administrative tribunals), legislation, books, journals, practice materials, newsletters, and encyclopedias such as the *Halsbury's Laws of Canada*.

Thomson Reuters Canada: Thomson Reuters Canada's products include Westlaw Edge Canada, Practical Law and other specialized services. They provide access to Canadian case law (from courts and administrative tribunals), legislation, journals, books, ad current awareness materials. Westlaw Edge includes publications like the *Canadian Abridgement* and the *Canadian Encyclopedic Digest*.

United Kingdom

British and Irish Legal Information Institute (https://www.bailii.org/, accessed May 26, 2022): British and Irish Legal Information Institute (BAILII) is a free database that provides access to case law, legislation, and Law Commission reports from the United Kingdom, England and Wales, Scotland, Northern Ireland, Jersey, Saint Helena, Ireland, and the European Union. The database features a listing of "Leading Cases by Subject," which have been selected by the legal academic community.

Incorporated Council of Law Reporting (ICLR Online): ICLR Online provides access to case law from England and Wales. It is the official reporter of the law reports series.

LexisLibrary: This is a subscription database, and it provides access to United Kingdom case law, legislation, forms, precedents, journals, commentaries, books, and encyclopedias such as the Halsbury's Laws series.

vLex: This database provides access to United Kingdom case law and legislation updated daily. Case law from this resource includes reported and unreported judgments.

Westlaw Edge UK: This database provides access to United Kingdom case law, legislation, journals, books, and precedents.

United States

There are many print and online sources available for finding law materials for the United States. While some of these sources, such as Westlaw, LexisNexis, Bloomberg Law, and HeinOnline, are subscription based, there are other free online databases, research guides, and governmental and nongovernmental websites that provide important primary and secondary materials. Several chapters, and in particular chapter 1, have already elaborated on the research process and finding specific resources. This section will, therefore, highlight some of the primary fee-based and free sources for locating United States legal materials. Some of the databases mentioned in this section have also been discussed in previous chapters.

Cases, Statutes, Secondary Sources, and Dockets

Westlaw, LexisNexis, and Bloomberg Law are subscription databases that provide access to cases, statutes, regulations, legislative history, dockets, and secondary materials such as law review articles, news, and other resources. In addition to its expansive collection of law journals, HeinOnline also contains historical materials and is also useful for legislative history research. These databases provide substantial coverage of both federal and state materials, but also some international law coverage. A newer database is Fastcase (https://www.fastcase.com/, accessed September 20, 2023), which provides similar coverage to Westlaw, LexisNexis, and Bloomberg Law. Fastcase has partnered with national, state, and county bar associations to provide access to its database as a benefit to members of these bars.

Google Scholar (https://scholar.google.com/, accessed September 20, 2023): In addition to providing access to articles, Google Scholar is also a free source for researching case law. There are options to search both state and federal courts. It allows filtering by date, and alerts can be created.

United States Supreme Court Documents: From the U.S. Supreme Court website (https://www.supremecourt.gov/, accessed May 30, 2022), there is access to opinions, oral arguments, filings and rules, and case documents. The official publication of the opinions of the Supreme Court is the *United States Reports*, or *U.S. Reports* (https://www.supremecourt.gov/, accessed May 30, 2022). The website currently has coverage from the 1991 Term (volume 502) through to the 2015 Term (volume 578, Part 1).

The Oyez Project (https://www.oyez.org/, accessed May 30, 2022) also facilitates research on Supreme Court cases, its justices, arguments, and Supreme Court news.

Georgetown Law Library Supreme Court Research Guide (https://guides.ll.georgetown.edu/supreme_court, accessed May 30, 2022).

Georgetown Law Library Supreme Court Nominations Research Guide (https://guides.ll.georgetown.edu/supreme_court_nominations, accessed May 30, 2022).

Bills, Public Laws, Hearings, and Committee Reports

Congress.gov (accessed May 30, 2022) provides access to bills, public laws, House and Senate documents, roll call votes, the United States Code, hearings, and committee reports. Searches can be filtered by specific Congresses. The *Congressional Record* is also available for searching. *The Daily Digest* (https://www.congress.gov/congressional-record, accessed May 30, 2022) is searchable by date or by the Congressional Record Index (https://www.congress.gov/congressional-record/congressional-record-index, accessed May 30, 2022).

Administrative Law Materials

In addition to using the above-mentioned subscription databases to find administrative law, the following sources are also important for locating these materials.

The Govinfo website provides access to the Code of Federal Regulations (CFR) (https://www.govinfo.gov/app/collection/cfr, accessed May 30, 2022).The CFR contains the codification of all the general and permanent rules of the departments and agencies of the federal government that have been published in the *Federal Register*. The CFR is divided into fifty titles covering a wide range of topics that are regulated. In a sense, its structure is similar to that of the United States Code.

From this website, there is also access to the eCFR (https://www.ecfr.gov/, accessed May 30, 2022), which is the online and regularly updated version of the print CFR.

The Federal Register (https://www.federalregister.gov/, accessed May 30, 2022), mentioned above, is updated daily and contains notices, rules, and proposed rules of departments and agencies, as well as presidential documents such as executive orders, proclamations, and memoranda. It allows for searching by agency, as well as via the Federal Register Index (https://www.federalregister.gov/index/2022, accessed May 30, 2022), which covers the years 2013–2022.

State Law Research

In addition to all of the above resources, the National Conference of State Legislatures website (https://www.ncsl.org/, accessed May 30, 2022) is invaluable for bill tracking (https://www.ncsl.org/research/telecommunications-and-information-technology/ncsl-50-state-searchable-bill-tracking-databases.aspx, accessed May 30, 2022) in the fifty states. It is useful for researching proposed legislation at the state level.

The Law Library of Congress (https://www.loc.gov/research-centers/law-library-of-congress/researcher-resources/databases/, accessed May 30, 2022) has also previously been mentioned as an important source not only for United States laws, but also foreign, comparative, and international law sources. Some of its materials include research guides, Guide to Law Online, and other legislative and statutory resources.

Other Resources

The Georgetown Law Library Research Guides link (https://guides.ll.georgetown.edu/home, accessed May 30, 2022) is useful because it contains resources for individual state law research and topical law research.

Civil Law Jurisdictions

China

ChinaLawInfo is a subscription-only database that provides access to Chinese laws, regulations, journals, and legal news. There are English translations of selected materials.

France

Légifrance (https://www.legifrance.gouv.fr/, accessed May 26, 2022) provides free access to French codes, case law, administrative documents, official publications, and Parliamentary debates.

Religious Legal Systems

Middle Eastern Countries

LexisNexis Middle East provides access to laws, gazettes, regulatory materials, current awareness materials, books, and practical guidance for countries in this region. It covers Bahrain, Egypt, Jordan, Kuwait, Lebanon, Morocco, Oman, Qatar, Saudi Arabia, Turkey, and the United Arab Emirates. They provide translation from Arabic to English for selected materials.

Mixed Legal Systems

Kenya

Kenya Laws (http://kenyalaw.org/kl/index.php?id=81, accessed May 26, 2022): Kenya Laws is the official publisher of *Kenya Law Reports* and the Laws of Kenya. This website provides access to case law, legislation, bills, and gazettes.

Nigeria

LexisNexis Africa provides access to the Laws of Nigeria and case law from Nigeria.

South Africa

Southern African Legal Information Institute (SafLII) (http://www.saflii.org.za/, accessed May 26, 2022) provides free access to case law, legislation, gazettes, court rules, and journals from South Africa. It also includes selected legal materials from countries in the region like Angola, Botswana, Mauritius, Mozambique, Swaziland, and Uganda.

Professional Associations

The activities of professional associations should not be underestimated in the career of professional librarians especially when working with foreign, comparative, and international research. This specialization, as we have discussed in this chapter, often requires finding and locating materials from other jurisdictions. Attending annual meetings or conferences of professional associations helps build lifelong networking opportunities with professional colleagues and peers. These associations facilitate and organize seminars, workshops, and training throughout the year to advance professional growth. Each of them has social media platforms, blogs, and listservs where they post and share useful information.

- American Association of Law Libraries (https://www.aallnet.org/, accessed May 26, 2022)
- American Society of International Law (https://www.asil.org/, accessed May 26, 2022)
- Australian Law Librarians' Association (https://www.alla.asn.au/, accessed May 26, 2022)
- British & Irish Association of Law Librarians (https://biall.org.uk/, accessed May 26, 2022)

- Canadian Association of Law Libraries (https://www.callacbd.ca/, accessed May 26, 2022)
- International Association of Law Libraries (https://iall.org/, accessed May 26, 2022)
- Organisation of South Africa Law Libraries (https://www.osall.org.za/, accessed May 26, 2022)

References

Armstrong, J. D. S., Knott, Christopher A., and Witt, R. Martin. *Where the Law Is: An Introduction to Advanced Legal Research*. St. Paul: West Academic Publishing, 2018.

Bhat, Ishwara P. *Ideas and Methods of Legal Research*. New Delhi: Oxford University Press, 2020. https://doi org.czproxy.library.yorku.ca/10.1093/oso/9780199493098.001.0001.

Bussani, Mauro, and Mattei, Ugo. *The Cambridge Companion to Comparative Law*. Cambridge: Cambridge University Press, 2012.

Doebbler, Curtis F. J. *Dictionary of Public International Law*. Lanham; Maryland: Rowman & Littlefield, 2018.

Fox, James R. *Dictionary of International and Comparative Law*. Dobbs Ferry, New York: Oceana Publications Inc., 1997.

Gutteridge, H. C. *Comparative Law: An Introduction to the Comparative Method of Legal Study and Research*. Cambridge: Cambridge University Press, 2015.

Hoffman, Marci, Ed. *Foreign Law Guide*. Leiden: Martinus Nijhoff, 2012.

Hoffman, Marci, and Rumsey, Mary. *International and Foreign Legal Research: A Coursebook*. Leiden: Martinus Nijhoff Publishers, 2012.

Olson, Kent C. *Legal Research in a Nutshell*. 14th edition. St. Paul: West Academic Publishing, 2021.

Olson, Kent C., Kirschenfeld, Aaron S., and Mattson, Ingrid. *Principles of Legal Research.* 3rd edition. St. Paul: West Academic Publishing, 2020.

O'Neill, Cara. *Legal Research: How to Find and Understand the Law.* 19th edition. Berkeley: NOLO Press, 2021.

Organization of American States. *Comparative Law Studies: Law and Legal Systems of the Commonwealth Caribbean States and Other Members of the Organization of American States.* Washington, DC: Organization of American States, 1987.

Roberts, Anthea. *Comparative International Law.* Oxford: Oxford University Press, 2018.

Siems, Mathias. *Comparative Law.* Cambridge: Cambridge University Press, 2022.

Sloan, Amy E. *Basic Legal Research: Tools and Strategies.* 8th edition. New York: Wolters Kluwer, 2021.

Steenken, Beau B., and Brooks, Tina M. *Sources of American Law: An Introduction to Legal Research*. 5th edition. Chicago: CALIeLangdell Press, 2021. (The online version of this book is available through The Center for Computer-Assisted Legal Instruction (CALI), subscription required: cali.org.)

Statute of the International Court of Justice. https://www.icj-cij.org/en/statute#CHAPTER_II (accessed June 15, 2021, and March 19, 2022).

Winer, Anthony S., et al. *International Law Legal Research.* Durham: Carolina Academic Press, 2013.

Chapter 12

Selected Emerging Legal Topics

This chapter discusses some emerging legal issues and assesses recent developments in existing areas of law. As is usually the case, the law often attempts to keep pace with new themes in the social, economic, political, and technology spheres. This is especially pronounced in the four newer or emerging areas of law that will be reviewed, namely cryptocurrencies, cannabis/marijuana, climate change, and space law/space tourism. The chapter will outline Caribbean and international legislation and landmark cases that are shaping these areas, as well as existing resources that can facilitate research on these topics.

Cannabis/Marijuana

Regionally, and internationally, cannabis/marijuana laws are undergoing changes, spurred on by calls for decriminalization and the development of the medical marijuana industry. Historically, marijuana, cannabis, or "ganja," as it is known in Jamaica, has been an important part of the Rastafarian religion, and this group has been at the forefront of calling for changes in marijuana laws. They have also borne the brunt of criminalization in the practice of their faith. Decriminalization has been evident in many parts of the world, and although there are still several places where there is reluctance to move in this direction, Caribbean governments are responding to these changes and are creating policies and amending legislation.

A CARICOM Regional Commission on Marijuana was formed, and at their 2018 meeting, the issued the report *Waiting to Exhale—Safeguarding Our Future Through Responsible Socio-Legal Policy on Marijuana* (https://caricom.org/documents/report-of-the-caricom-regional-commission-on-marijuana-2018-waiting-to-exhale-safeguarding-our-future-through-responsible-socio-legal-policy-on-marijuana/, accessed January 26, 2022). Chair of the CARICOM Regional Commission on Marijuana, Professor Rose-Marie Belle Antoine, noted that the report arose out of the 2014 CARICOM Heads of Government meeting with the aim of "reform of the legal regimes regulating cannabis/marijuana in CARICOM countries." Other initiatives include the EU-CARICOM Law Conference: Marijuana and the Law; the establishment by Jamaica of a Cannabis Task Force; and the subsequent amendment of its Dangerous Drugs Act to decriminalize marijuana.

Climate Change

There are already strong indications of climate change with rising seas because of global warming. The small island developing states of the Caribbean are among the most vulnerable countries, given the frequency of natural disasters such as hurricanes, earthquakes, and volcanoes, and their impact on the region's economy. Although the region does not rank high as a greenhouse producer, it nevertheless would be among the most negatively impacted by climate change. Tourism is the main contributor to the region's economy, and therefore, the threat of climate change is a major preoccupation for Caribbean governments. The Organization of American States has been active in planning for climate change and has established several projects, starting with the Caribbean Planning for Adaptation to Climate Change from as far back as 2001, and has built on that project with several others. CARICOM's

Caribbean Community Climate Change Centre was established in 2002 and is based in Belize. It provides guidelines and assistance with climate change policy for CARICOM member states.

One useful resource for tracking climate change laws is the Climate Change Laws of the World database (https://climate-laws.org/, accessed May 30, 2022), which is a collaboration of the London School of Economics Grantham Research Institute, and the Sabin Center at Columbia University Law School. The database facilitates searches for global climate laws, policies, and cases. Search options include date of legislation, date of last change, sector, instruments, and frameworks. With respect to cases, searches can be done by jurisdiction, party types, date case started, and date of last change. This is a very comprehensive database that researchers of Caribbean climate change cases, laws, and policies would find useful.

Cryptocurrencies

Cryptocurrencies have been steadily gaining interest and momentum in the Caribbean, with the anticipation of economic growth from this emerging sector. Governments in the region are attempting to keep abreast of the rapid development by regulating cryptocurrencies, in keeping with policies and approaches in other regions of the world. Hesitancy by governments to move on either adoption of cryptocurrencies or in drafting legislation appears to be linked to concerns about terrorism as well as the need to protect consumers. Strong interest in cryptocurrency policies and legislation has also come from the Caribbean Tourism Organisation, in light of the importance of tourism in Caribbean economies. Several Caribbean states and the Eastern Caribbean Central Bank have leaned toward making their Central Bank Digital Currency (CBDC) legal tender. CBDCs are a stable approach in that they are government backed.

Currently, there are varying stages of legislative developments in Caribbean territories, and this section will provide an overview of the current status in the region and also scan the regional and international landscapes to assess the pace of cryptocurrency legislation and policy beyond the Caribbean. Since this is a very fluid topic, it is best to consult the official government websites for up-to-date laws. CARICOM (https://caricom.org/, accessed May 30, 2022) is also an important resource for regional updates on this topic. In addition, chapter 11 provides more details on sources for foreign, comparative, and international law research.

With respect to the Organisation of Eastern Caribbean States, there are plans for a pilot of a CBDC in four countries that are members of the Eastern Caribbean Currency Union. These states are Antigua and Barbuda, Grenada, St. Kitts and Nevis, and St. Lucia. Antigua and Barbuda also passed the Digital Asset Business Bill in 2020. The bill requires companies dealing in cryptocurrencies to be licensed. The bill extends regulation to companies providing payment and exchange services. Below is a summary of developments in Caribbean states where cryptocurrency policies and legislation have advanced, followed by resources that are useful for researching regional and global cryptocurrency legislation.

Anguilla

In 2017, Anguilla proposed the Anguilla Utility Token Offering Act to regulate cryptocurrency.

The Bahamas

The Securities Commission of the Bahamas completed a draft of the Digital Assets and Registered Exchanges Bill in 2020.

Barbados

Barbados does not currently regulate cryptocurrency. However, the Barbados Central Bank and its Financial Service Commission took the first steps by establishing a Regulatory Sandbox, which allows companies to explore and test innovations.

British Virgin Islands

Although there is no cryptocurrency legislation in the British Virgin Islands, there is an interest, and several preparatory steps have been taken there. The Financial Services Commission has also been providing guidance on and oversight of this sector.

Jamaica

After a successful pilot by the Bank of Jamaica, which lasted from May to December 2021, Jamaica moved toward the launch of its digital currency in the first quarter of 2022. Currently, however, there is no legislation in place.

Africa and the Middle East

Africa

Cryptocurrency adoption and legislation in Africa are mixed, with some countries warning against cryptocurrencies and some taking tentative steps to integrate them into their economies. At the moment, South Africa appears to lead the continent in advancements in cryptocurrency adoption. The African Union website (https://au.int/, accessed May 30, 2022) is a key resource for legislation, reports, and economic policies. For developments in West Africa, the Economic Commission of West African States (https://www.ecowas.int/, accessed May 30, 2022) is also an important source. Since cryptocurrency laws and policies are fluid, it is best to visit specific government websites for individual country progress in this area of law.

Middle East

There is limited adoption of cryptocurrencies in the Middle East. However, some central banks in the region are exploring their own digital currencies. Bahrain and the United Arab Emirates (UAE) appear to be more advanced with legislation. In 2019 the Central Bank of Bahrain (https://www.cbb.gov.bh/laws-regulations/, accessed May 30, 2022) outlined cryptocurrency regulations. The

UAE is a federal state and comprises seven emirates. Banking and financial regulation are handled at the federal level. The UAE Central Bank (https://www.centralbank.ae/en, accessed May 30, 2022) is useful for an overview of banking policies. The UAE Central Bank also has a link to Laws and Regulations (https://www.centralbank.ae/en/laws-and-regulations, accessed May 30, 2022).

Asia, Australia, and New Zealand

Asia

Cryptocurrency legislations lag in China, Hong Kong, Malaysia, Thailand, and Vietnam and appear to be progressing in Indonesia, Japan, and Singapore. Indonesia has passed BAPPEBTI Regulation No. 5 (2019) and BAPPEBTI Regulation No. 7 (2020) aimed at providing a legal framework for cryptocurrencies. Japan passed the Payment Services Act in 2009. The Monetary Authority of Singapore regulates cryptocurrencies, and Singapore also passed their Payment Services Act in 2019.

Australia

Australia is working on the establishment of a licensing structure and the eventual development of a Central Bank Digital Currency in 2022. The Australian Securities and Investment Commission (https://asic.gov.au/, accessed May 30, 2022) is an important resource on cryptocurrency policies.

New Zealand

Currently, cryptocurrencies are not regulated in New Zealand. The Reserve Bank of New Zealand (https://www.rbnz.govt.nz/, accessed May 30, 2022) is the country's central bank and provides information on monetary policies and regulations. The central bank's Regulatory Developments link (https://www.rbnz.govt.nz/regulation-and-supervision/our-oversight-of-financial-market-infrastructures/developing-the-legislative-framework-for-financial-market-infrastructures, accessed May 30, 2022) provides updates on new policies and regulatory decisions.

European Union and the United Kingdom

European Union

The European Union Regulation, Markets in Crypto Assets (MiCA) has already passed through its first readings in both the Council and European Parliament. The regulation will support the EU's Digital Finance Strategy. EUR-Lex (https://eur-lex.europa.eu/legal-content/EN/TXT/?uri=CELEX%3A52020PC0593, accessed May 30, 2022) provides the full text of MiCA. The European Central Bank (https://www.ecb.europa.eu/home/html/index.en.html, accessed May 30, 2022) and the European Banking Authority (https://www.eba.europa.eu/, accessed May 30, 2022) are two good sources for current policies and regulations.

United Kingdom

In the United Kingdom, the Financial Conduct Authority (FCA) (https://www.fca.org.uk/, accessed May 30, 2022) is one of the main bodies providing guidance on cryptocurrencies, or crypto assets. Its Publications section (https://www.fca.org.uk/publications, accessed May 30, 2022) contains a number of reports and policy statements that are useful. In 2019, it issued PS 19/22, its Guidance on Cryptoassets (https://www.fca.org.uk/publications/policy-statements/ps19-22-guidance-cryptoassets, accessed May 30, 2022). The HM Treasury (https://www.gov.uk/government/organisations/hm-treasury), Bank of England (https://www.bankofengland.co.uk/), and the Scottish Reserve Bank (https://www.reservebank.scot/#gsc.tab=0, all accessed May 30, 2022) are additional resources for guidance on monetary policy developments.

A Crypto Assets Task Force was created in 2018, which includes HM Treasury, Bank of England, and the FCA. The main objective is to determine the regulation of this sector.

Central and South America

In Central and South America, there are varied responses to the regulation of cryptocurrencies. However, the situation, as in other parts of the world, is fluid. To date, Bitcoin is illegal in Bolivia and Ecuador, whereas in Nicaragua and Costa Rica, it is not. Regulation of cryptocurrencies also appears to be lagging in Brazil, Chile, and Colombia. Venezuela has made advances with state backing of Petro.

North America

Canada

Cryptocurrency and other securities laws in Canada are enacted by the provinces and territories, rather than at the federal level. However, the Canadian Securities Administrators (CSA) (https://www.securities-administrators.ca/, accessed May 30, 2022) plays a coordinating role. The CSA's Regulatory Sandbox page (https://www.securities-administrators.ca/resources/regulatory-sandbox/, accessed May 30, 2022) provides some guidance on securities and technological development.

United States

The Securities and Exchange Commission (https://www.sec.gov/, accessed May 30, 2022) regulates cryptocurrencies in the United States. Its Regulatory Actions page (https://www.sec.gov/page/regulation, accessed May 30, 2022) provides information on proposed rules, final rules, and policy statements. The Laws that Govern the Securities Industry link (https://www.investor.gov/introduction-investing/investing-basics/role-sec/laws-govern-securities-industry, accessed May 30, 2022) is also helpful in tracing the development of securities laws in the United States. The Federal Reserve Board website (https://www.federalreserve.gov/, accessed May 30, 2022) also had a wealth of publications to facilitate research on this topic.

The National Conference of State Legislatures (https://www.ncsl.org/about-us, accessed May 30, 2022) has previously been highlighted, and it is a very useful place to research the laws of individual states. They have provided a state-by-state breakdown of Cryptocurrency 2021 Legislation (https://www.ncsl.org/research/financial-services-and-commerce/cryptocurrency-2021-legislation, accessed May 30, 2022).

Space Law/Space Tourism

Space law is not a very new area of law. However, recent developments related to space law, such as commercial space travel and space tourism, have raised legal issues such as liability, environmental problems related to debris in space, among other concerns. New commercial ventures in space tourism, by companies such as Blue Origin and SpaceX, the companies owned by billionaires Jeff Bezos and Elon Musk, respectively, provide the opportunity for private citizens who can afford it to travel to space. There are, therefore, new players in the space research and travel sectors, in addition to previous governmental agencies such as NASA (USA), ROSCOSMOS (Russian Federation), ISRO (India), CNSA (China), and ESA (United Kingdom).

The Caribbean, due to its size and limited economic resources, has not yet developed a substantial case law in this area. However, it is important to have an awareness of the main resources available to research space law and space tourism.

References

Cannabis/Marijuana Law

General

Alovisetti, Charles S., and Furman, Cassia. *The Cannabis Business: Understanding Law, Finance, and Governance in America's Newest Industry*. New York: Routledge, 2021.

American Bar Association. *The Marijuana Law Sourcebook*. Chicago: American Bar Association, 2015.

Berman, Douglas A., and Kreit, Alex. *Marijuana Law and Policy*. Durham: Carolina Academic Press, 2020.

Bernstein, Austin, and Turcott, Bruce. *Cannabis Law Deskbook*. Aurora: Thomson Reuters, 2021.

Cohen, Barak, and Bleicher, Michael. *Cannabis Law: A Primer on Federal and State Law Regarding Marijuana, Hemp, and CBD*. Chicago: American Bar Association, 2021.

Decorte, Tom, Lenton, Simon, and Wilkins, Chris. *Legalizing Cannabis: Experiences, Lessons and Scenarios*. Abingdon: Routledge, 2021.

Fichtelman, Carol A. *Marijuana Law: A Legal Research Guide*. Getzville: William S. Hein & Co., 2021.

Halsey, Anna, Kaufman, Greg, Shah, Meghana, and Worthy, Virginia. *The State of Cannabis Law: A Fifty State Compendium*. New York: Wolters Kluwer, 2020.

Jones, Karin D., and Shore, James M. *Marijuana Regulation*. New York: LexisNexis, 2023.

MacFarlane, Bruce. *Cannabis Law: The Legislative Framework*. Toronto: Thomson Reuters, 2020.

Malek, Shabnam. *Cannabis: Business Fundamentals 2022*. New York: Practising Law Institute, 2022.

Mikoley, Kate. *The Marijuana Legalization Debate*. New York: Cavendish Square Publishing, 2022.

Mikos, Robert A. *Marijuana Law, Policy, and Authority*. New York: Wolters Kluwer, 2017.

Mosehr, Clayton James, and Akins, Scott. *In the Weeds: Demonization, Legalization, and the Evolution of U.S. Marijuana Policy*. Philadelphia: Temple University Press, 2019.

Osbeck, Mark K., and Bromberg, Howard. *Marijuana Law in a Nutshell*. St Paul: West Academic Publishing, 2022.

Seddon, Toby. *Regulating Cannabis: A Global Review and Future Directions*. Cham: Palgrave Macmillan, 2021.

Government and Intergovernmental Resources

CARICOM. Documents and Publications. https://caricom.org/documents-and-publications/ (accessed May 30, 2022).

National Conference of State Legislatures. State Medical Cannabis Laws. https://www.ncsl.org/research/health/state-medical-marijuana-laws.aspx (accessed May 30, 2022).

United Nations Office on Drugs and Crime. https://www.unodc.org/ (accessed May 30, 2022).

Journals

Cannabis Law Journal. https://journal.cannabislaw.report/ (accessed May 30, 2022).

Journal of Cannabis Research. https://jcannabisresearch.biomedcentral.com/about (accessed May 30, 2022).

Legal Databases

Westlaw: In the Emerging Areas of Practice Series database, there is a section called Cannabis Law. However, login is required.

Research Guides, Blogs, and General Initiatives

Drexel University. https://drexellaw.libguides.com/cannabis (accessed May 30, 2022).

Lewis and Clark Law School. https://library.lclark.edu/c.php?g=978881&p=7078464 (accessed May 30, 2022).

Rutgers University. https://libguides.rutgers.edu/marijuana (accessed May 30, 2022).

Texas State Law Library. Cannabis and the Law. https://guides.sll.texas.gov/cannabis/general-information (accessed May 30, 2022).

Climate Change

General

Birchler, Alexandra. *Climate Change, Resulting Natural Disasters and the Legal Responsibilities of States: An International Law Perspective.* Cambridge: Intersentia Ltd., 2020.

Bodansky, Daniel, Brunnee, Jutta, and Rajamani, Lavanya. *International Climate Change Law*. Oxford: Oxford University Press, 2017.

Farber, Daniel A., and Carlarne, Cinnamon Pinon. *Climate Change Law*. Eagan: Foundation Press, 2023.

Lord, Richard. *Climate Change Liability: Transnational Law and Practice*. Cambridge: Cambridge University Press, 2012.

Posner, Eric A., and Weisbach, David A. *Climate Change Justice*. Princeton: Princeton University Press, 2015.

Quirico, Ottavio, and Boumghar, Mouloud. *Climate Change and Human Rights: An International and Comparative Law Perspective*. London: Routledge, 2018.

Richardson, Benjamin J. *Local Climate Change Law: Environmental Regulation in Cities and Other Localities.* Cheltenham: Edward Elgar, 2012.

Robinson, Nicholas A., Wang, Xi, Harmon, Lin, and Wegnueller, Sarah. *Dictionary of Environmental and Climate Change Law.* Cheltenham: Edward Elgar, 2015.

Van Calster, Geert. *Research Handbook on Climate Change Mitigation Law.* Cheltenham: Edward Elgar Publishing, 2016.

Wold, Chris, Hunter, David, and Powers, Melissa. 2013. *Climate Change and the Law.* 2nd ed. New Providence: LexisNexis, 2013.

Zahar, Alexander. *International Climate Change Law and State Compliance*. Abingdon: Routledge, 2016.

Government and Intergovernmental Resources

Intergovernmental Panel on Climate Change. https://www.ipcc.ch/ (accessed May 30, 2022).

National Conference of State Legislatures. Climate and Energy Legislation Tracking. https://www.ncsl.org/research/energy/climate-and-energy (accessed May 30, 2022).

United Nations Environment Programme. https://www.unep.org/ (accessed May 30, 2022).

World Meteorological Organization:. https://public.wmo.int/en (accessed May 30, 2022).

Journals

Climate. https://www.mdpi.com/journal/climate (accessed May 30, 2022).

Climate Policy. https://www.tandfonline.com/toc/tcpo20/current (accessed May 30, 2022).

Energy and Climate Change. https://www.sciencedirect.com/journal/energy-and-climate-change (accessed May 30, 2022).

Journal of Climate. https://www.ametsoc.org/index.cfm/ams/publications/journals/journal-of-climate/ (accessed May 30, 2022).

Research Guides, Blogs, and General Initiatives

Georgetown University. Climate Change Guide. https://guides.library.georgetown.edu/climate (accessed May 30, 2022).

Globalex. Global Warming—Researching the U.S. Approach to the U.N. Framework Convention on Climate Change and the Kyoto Protocol. https://www.nyulawglobal.org/globalex/Climate_Change_Kyoto_Protocol1.html (accessed May 30, 2022).

London School of Economics/Columbia University Law School. Climate Change Laws of the World. https://climate-laws.org/ (accessed May 30, 2022).

New York University Law School's Caribbean Climate Justice Initiative. https://chrgj.org/focus-areas/climate-and-environment/caribbean-climate-justice-initiative/ (accessed May 30, 2022).

World Bank: Climate Change Action Plan, 2021–2025 (accessed September 30, 2023).

Cryptocurrencies

General

Artzt, Matthias, and Richter, Thomas. *Handbook of Blockchain Law: A Guide to Understanding and Resolving the Legal Challenges of the Blockchain Technology*. Frederick: Wolters Kluwer, 2020.

Cappiello, Benedetta, and Carullo, Gherardo. *Blockchain Law and Governance*. Cham: Springer, 2021.

Chohan, Usman W. *Assessing the Differences in Cryptocurrency Legality Across National Jurisdictions*. Discussion Paper Series. Notes on the 21st Century. https://papers.ssrn.com/sol3/papers.cfm?abstract_id=3042248 (accessed March 8, 2022).

De Filippi, Primavera. *Blockchain and the Law: The Rule of Code*. Cambridge: Harvard University Press, 2018.

Dewey, Josias N. (ed). *Blockchain and Cryptocurrency Regulation*. 3rd ed. London: Global Legal Group Ltd., 2020.

Fox, David, Green, Sarah, and Carr, Daniel J. *Cryptocurrencies in Public and Private Law*. Oxford: Oxford University Press, 2019.

Futter, Dror, and Wright, Aaron. *Blockchain 2.0: 2021 Legal and Regulatory Developments*. New York: Practising Law Institute, 2021.

Girasa, Rosario J. *Regulation of Cryptocurrencies and Blockchain Technologies: National and International Perspectives*. Cham: Palgrave Macmillan, 2018.

Haynes, Andrew, and Yeoh, Peter. *Cryptocurrencies and Cryptoassets: Regulatory and Legal Issues*. Abingdon: Routledge, 2020.

Herian, Robert. *Regulating Blockchain. Critical Perspectives in Law and Technology*. Abingdon: Routledge, 2020.

Hutchinson, Allan C. *Cryptocurrencies and the Regulatory Challenge*. Abingdon: Routledge, 2022.

Kerrigan, Charles. *Cryptocurrency and Blockchain Law and Regulation*. London: Sweet and Maxwell, 2023.

Law Library of Congress. *Regulation of Cryptocurrency in Selected Jurisdictions*. Washington, D.C.: Law Library of Congress, Global Research Center, 2018.

Lee, Joseph. *Crypto-Finance, Law and Regulation: Governing an Emerging Ecosystem*. Abingdon: Routledge, 2022.

Markham, Jerry W. *Cryptocurrency Regulation: A Primer*. Cheltenham: Edward Elgar Publishing, 2023.

Shipkevich, Felix. *Digital Coins and Cryptocurrencies Law and Regulation: Cases and Problems*. Durham: Carolina Academic Press, 2023.

Stabile, Daniel T., Prior, Kimberly A., and Hinkes, Andrew M. *Digital Assets and Blockchain Technology: U.S. Law and Regulation*. Cheltenham: Edward Elgar Publishing, 2020.

Swan, Edward J. *Cryptocurrency Law: A Guide to Digital Asset Regulation Around the World*. Frederick: Kluwer Law International, 2023.

Symons, Ben. *Cryptocurrency and Blockchain*. London: Bloomsbury Professional, 2020.

Vandezande, Niels. *Virtual Currencies. A Legal Framework*. Cambridge: Intersentia, 2018.

Government and Intergovernmental Resources

Financial Stability Board. https://www.fsb.org/ (accessed May 30, 2022).

National Conference of State Legislatures. Cryptocurrency 2021 Legislation. https://www.ncsl.org/research/financial-services-and-commerce/cryptocurrency-2021-legislation.aspx (accessed May 30, 2022).

U.S. Securities and Exchange Commission. https://www.sec.gov/ (accessed May 30, 2022).

Journals

Cryptoeconomic Systems. MIT. https://cryptoeconomicsystems.pubpub.org/ (accessed May 30, 2022).

International Journal of Blockchain Law.

Stanford Journal of Blockchain Law and Policy. https://stanford-jblp.pubpub.org/ (accessed May 30, 2022).

Research Guides, Blogs, and General Initiatives

Boston University. https://library.bu.edu/blockchain_cryptocurrencies (accessed May 30, 2022).

Law Library of Congress. https://blogs.loc.gov/law/2020/10/united-states-blockchain-and-cryptocurrency-resources/ (accessed May 30, 2022).

Westlaw

The Blockchain: A Guide for Legal and Business Professionals. 2016. (Login required).

Space Law/Space Tourism

General

Abeyratne, Ruwantissa. *Space Security Law*. Heidelberg: Springer, 2014.

Benko, Marietta, Schrogl, Kai-Uwe, Digrell, Denise, and Jolley, Esther. *Space Law: Current Problems and Perspectives for Future Regulation*. Utrecht: Eleven International Publishing, 2005.

Bhat, B. Sandeepa. *Space Law in the Era of Commercialisation*. Lucknow: Eastern Book Company, 2010.

Bhat, B. Sandeepa. *Space Law: The Emerging Trends: On the Occasion of Celebrating the 50th Anniversary of Outer Space Treaty*. Kolkata: Eastern Law House, 2018.

Chatzipanagiotis, Michael. *The Legal Status of Space Tourists in the Framework of Commercial Suborbital Flights*. Koln: Carl Heymanns Verlag 2011.

Diederiks-Verschoor, Isabella Henrietta Philepina, and Kopal, Vladimir. *An Introduction to Space Law*. Frederick: Aspen Publishers, 2008.

Failat, Yanal Abul, and Ferreira-Snyman, Anel. *Outer Space Law: Legal Policy and Practice*. 2nd ed. London: Global Law and Business, 2022.

Harrington, Andrea. *Space Insurance and the Law: Maximizing Private Activities in Outer Space*. Cheltenham: Edward Elgar Publishing, 2021.

Hobe, Stephan. *Space Law*. Oxford: Hart Publishing, 2020.

Kleiman, Matthew J. *The Little Book of Space Law*. Chicago: American Bar Association, Section of Science and Technology Law, 2013.

Lyall, Francis, and Larsen, Paul B. *Space Law: A Treatise*. London: Routledge, 2020.

Malinowska, Katarzyna. *Space Insurance: International Legal Aspects*. Alphen aan den Rijn: Wolters Kluwer, 2017.

Oduntan, Gbenga. *Sovereignty and Jurisdiction in Airspace and Outer Space: Legal Criteria for Spatial Delimitation*. London: Routledge, 2012. (Also available as an e-book.)

Rao, R. Venkata, Gopalkrishnan, V., and Abhjeet, Kumar. *Recent Development in Space Law: Opportunities and Challenges*. Singapore: Springer, 2018.

von der Dunk, Frans G. *International Space Law*. Cheltenham: Edward Elgar Publishing, 2018.

Wouters, Jan, De Man, Phillip, and Hansen, Rik. *Commercial Uses of Space and Space Tourism: Legal and Policy Aspects*. Cheltenham: Edward Elgar Publishing, 2019.

Government and Intergovernmental Resources

The London Institute of Space Policy and Law. https://www.space-institute.org/ (accessed May 30, 2022).

NASA.gov. https://www.nasa.gov/ (accessed May 30, 2022).

United Nations Office for Outer Space Affairs. https://www.unoosa.org/oosa/en/aboutus/index.html (accessed May 30, 2022).

Journals

Advanced Space Law. http://asljournal.org/ (accessed May 30, 2022).

Air and Space Law. Kluwer Law. https://kluwerlawonline.com/Journals/Air+and+Space+Law/18 (accessed May 30, 2022).

Annals of Air and Space Law. McGill University. https://www.mcgill.ca/iasl/annals (accessed May 30, 2022).

Studies in Space Law. https://brill.com/view/serial/SLAW (accessed May 30, 2022).

Research Guides, Blogs, and General Initiatives

Bodleian Libraries, University of Oxford. International Law: Air and Space. https://libguides.bodleian.ox.ac.uk/law-internat/as (accessed May 30, 2022).

Peace Palace Library. Space Law. https://peacepalacelibrary.nl/research-guide/space-law (accessed May 30, 2022).

University of Connecticut Law Library. Outer Space Law https://libguides.law.uconn.edu/c.php?g=1047257 (accessed May 30, 2022).

Appendix A

Caribbean Law School Libraries

The Bahamas:

Eugene Dupuch Law School Library: http://eugenedupuchlaw.edu.bs/library/ (accessed May 30, 2022).

Barbados:

Faculty of Law Library, Cave Hill Campus: https://www.cavehill.uwi.edu/lawlibrary/home.aspx (accessed May 30, 2022).

Cayman Islands:

Truman Bodden Law School Library: https://www.caymanlawschool.ky/library.html (accessed May 30, 2022).

Guyana:

University of Guyana. Department of Law: https://fss.uog.edu.gy/department-law (accessed May 30, 2022). Note: At the date of publication, this website was under development, and there is no link yet to the law library. However, it was useful to list this additional law school link.

Jamaica:

Norman Manley Law School Library, Jamaica: http://nmls.edu.jm/library/ (accessed May 30, 2022).

University of Technology, Jamaica: https://www.utech.edu.jm/academics/colleges-faculties/fol (accessed May 30, 2022). The University of Technology started its bachelor of laws (LLB) program in 2008. At the time of writing this book, law faculty does not appear to have a separate law library, but rather is served by the main Calvin McKain Library (https://www.utech.edu.jm/campus-experience/library/history, accessed May 30, 2022).

University of the Commonwealth Caribbean Law Library: https://www.ucc.edu.jm/library (accessed May 30, 2022).

Trinidad and Tobago:

Hugh Wooding Law School Library: http://www.hwls.edu.tt/library/ (accessed May 30, 2022).

Appendix B

Caribbean Law Research Guides

Caribbean Law Project; http.//www.commonlii.org/resources/55912.html (accessed May 30, 2022).

Commonwealth Caribbean Law Research Guide: https://guides.law.fsu.edu/caribbean (accessed May 30, 2022).

Guide to Caribbean Law Research: http://www.nyulawglobal.org/globalex/Caribbean1.html (accessed May 30, 2022).

Guyana Law and Legal Research: https://www.nyulawglobal.org/globalex/Guyana.html (accessed May 30, 2022).

The Caribbean Court of Justice: A Research Guide: https://www.llrx.com/2008/02/the-caribbean-court-of-justice-a-research-guide/ (accessed May 30, 2022).

The Jamaican Legal System and Legal Research: https://www.nyulawglobal.org/globalex/Jamaica1.html (accessed May 30, 2022).

Trinidad and Tobago Law and Legal Research: https://www.nyulawglobal.org/globalex/Trinidad_Tobago1.html (accessed May 30, 2022).

Index